"Even before sin and sorrow entered the world, God said that it is not good for people to be alone. Perhaps more than ever in our lifetimes, the past few years have brought this 'not-goodness' into the forefront with things like pandemic-induced social distancing, polarization, and dismantling of communities. But even in times such as these, Scripture holds out to us the promise of a friend who is born even for adversity, and who at all times sticks closer to us even than a brother (Prov. 17:17; 18:24). That friend, Jesus tells us, is none other than himself. In this hopeful book, Jared does a wonderful job helping us access our Lord in this most intimate way."

Scott Sauls, senior pastor of Christ Presbyterian Church and author of *Jesus Outside the Lines* and *Beautiful People Don't Just Happen*

"The odds are good that you make less of friendship than you ought. But you were made for it—and not just friendship with others but friendship with Christ himself. I so respect the way Jared C. Wilson unpacks the truth of what the friendship of Jesus is like and how it provides something for our souls we won't find anywhere but with him. Read this one twice."

Russ Ramsey, pastor and author of *Rembrandt Is in the Wind*

"Jared's writing always leaves me edified, refreshed, and more sure of the joy and hope I have in Jesus—*Friendship with the Friend of Sinners* is no exception. In a culture where true friendship is distorted, we need a better understanding of what it means to have a friend in the living Christ. This book will encourage the lonely and the lowly, pointing them to the best friend they can ever have."

Emily Jensen, coauthor of *Risen Motherhood* and author of *He Is Strong*

"If you've ever felt alone, isolated, ignored, or 'too much' for the people in your life, take heart. If you are struggling or floundering with relationships, be encouraged. Jared C. Wilson has written a book for you—for each of us—reminding us of the blessing and power we find in friendship with the Savior. This book methodically chipped away at my instinctively hard heart, exposing a tenderness that moved me to both tears and laughter as I reveled in the goodness we have in our dear friend, Jesus. Read this book, and then give it to everyone you know who needs a friend."

Steve Bezner, senior pastor of Houston Northwest Church

"I've been waiting for this book by Jared C. Wilson for years. He is the best author I know to write it, and I trust many will soon see why. The truth that God really does love us and we can know him is, I believe, the secret to the universe (and all of our hopes and worries). Exploring how we can know God through Jesus as friend is the remarkable key that unlocks the door to that secret—but sadly it is often overlooked or forgotten. Never fear; Jared has come with this book and, as a friend to you and me, hands us the key and invites us to enter. Come, one and all, and taste and see why Jesus is good and the best of friends."

Jason G. Duesing, provost of Midwestern Seminary and author of *Mere Hope*

"Friendship is tricky to define in a digital age—but what about friendship with Jesus? How do we define a relationship with a person we cannot see? Jared C. Wilson has given us a beautiful picture of friendship with our Savior, one that is neither too familiar nor too far off. Christ's friendship with us is vast and comforting, and this book is a balm to anyone longing to see friendship in its truest form."

Courtney Reissig, author of *Teach Me to Feel*

FRIENDSHIP WITH THE FRIEND OF SINNERS

The Remarkable Possibility
of Closeness with Christ

JARED C. WILSON

BakerBooks
a division of Baker Publishing Group
Grand Rapids, Michigan

Published by Baker Books
a division of Baker Publishing Group
Grand Rapids, Michigan
www.bakerbooks.com

Printed in the United States of America

Library of Congress Cataloging-in-Publication Data
Names: Wilson, Jared C., 1975– author.
Title: Friendship with the friend of sinners : the remarkable possibility of closeness with Christ / Jared C. Wilson.
Description: Grand Rapids, Michigan : Baker Books, a division of Baker Publishing Group, [2023] | Includes bibliographical references.
Identifiers: LCCN 2022061913 | ISBN 9781540901354 (paperback) | ISBN 9781540903204 (casebound) | ISBN 9781493441143 (ebook)
Subjects: LCSH: Friendship—Religious aspects—Christianity. | Jesus Christ—Person and offices. | Jesus Christ—Friends and associates.
Classification: LCC BV4647.F7 W56 2023 | DDC 241/.6762—dc23/eng/20230203
LC record available at https://lccn.loc.gov/2022061913

The author is represented by the literary agency of The Gates Group Agency.

Baker Publishing Group publications use paper produced from sustainable forestry practices and post-consumer waste whenever possible.

23   24   25   26   27   28   29   7   6   5   4   3   2   1

For the Thinklings—
Bill, Bird, Blo, and Phil

CONTENTS

I do not call you servants anymore, because a servant doesn't know what his master is doing. I have called you friends, because I have made known to you everything I have heard from my Father.

John 15:15

INTRODUCTION

Have you ever been so lonely you could die?

I have.

There's a good kind of solitude. The kind that's refreshing and renewing. The kind that allows a body to recharge and a mind to reset. There's the "getting away it from all" kind of aloneness that's healthy for a soul normally drowning in busyness and overstimulation.

And then there's the kind of solitude that brings with it an overwhelming feeling of desolation. It's a feeling of abandonment. You don't even have to be literally alone to feel it. You could be in a crowded room, at a party, with your family, even at church. No matter the circumstances, your *heart* is lonely.

It's a feeling akin to depression. Maybe you feel like nobody cares. Maybe you feel like people might care, but they don't really understand. Maybe they understand, but they can't do anything to help. Even the people who want to fix you can't fix you.

That's the kind of aloneness that's hard to climb out of. It's oppressive and suffocating.

More and more people suffer from this kind of loneliness every day. Our world, with no lack of relational outlets and social connections, virtual and otherwise, is nevertheless stifling under an epidemic of loneliness. It's an aloneness of the soul.

I have more than a few friends who have suffered from this affliction. I've been heartbroken to hear them recount their struggles. I've been surprised by these revelations too, though I shouldn't be, given my own struggles. I've wondered how I didn't notice, why I didn't know. I've been hurt that they didn't reach out for help. I say to them, "I wish I'd known! I would've been there for you."

But I know from experience that when you're in the midst of such darkness, it's hard to believe even your closest friends can help or would want to. *They couldn't do anything, even if they wanted to*, I've said to myself. *Plus, I don't want to burden them.*

Nobody wants to be the friend who brings their friends down.

So we bear the burden alone. And the weight of it begins to play tricks on our minds. We aren't just alone; we feel insignificant. We aren't just forgotten; we feel forsaken.

I've wrestled with this feeling off and on throughout my life. I was an insecure, neurotic kid. I'll share some reasons for that with you later in this book, but for now it's enough to say that I have always struggled with feeling *disapproved of*, with wanting to be known and understood and at the same time loved and accepted, but believing it wasn't possible. And then, when I finally did find someone who loved me and accepted me, I made a miserable mess of the whole thing.

I brought a world of sinful habits and toxic behaviors into my marriage, mainly through the use of pornography. I tried to keep these sins hidden, but I couldn't manage it for very long. Eventually, my ongoing, unrepentant betrayal blew up in my face. My marriage was wrecked. I was utterly alone again.

While my wife did not divorce me, we lived like roommates in our home. I slept in the guest bedroom and walked through each day like a zombie, plunged into deep depression and despair. I thought often about taking my own life.

This was the worst experience of my life, but believe it or not, it was in this soul-shriveling battle for hope that I rediscovered a soul-filling faith. These are the kinds of times faith is really made for, after all. As long as life is comfortable and convenient, we can make do with a comfortable and convenient Christianity. As long as life is easy, we can manage with an easy-believism. But in our lowest moments, a superficial faith won't hack it.

During that time, for about a year, I vacillated between an inconsolable sadness and a dangerous numbness. I spent countless nights facedown on the floor of that guest bedroom, begging God to do something for me. To do what? I wasn't sure. I just knew I needed him to fix it. (You pray totally differently when you feel your very life is at stake.) I had come to the end of my rope.

And then one night, circumstantially no different from any of the previous nights, something different happened. I was crying into the carpet as I had hundreds of times before, pleading with God to help me, and there was a change. I felt as if God reached through the roof into that room and grabbed me in his hand. I was reminded of the message of the gospel, the good news that God loves even sinners like me and that God approves even of sinners like me because of the saving work of Jesus. It wasn't a message I didn't know. It wasn't a message I hadn't heard before. But I heard it that night *as if for the first time*.

In a very real way, at the moment I most deserved to be utterly alone and rejected, Jesus came into that room, sat on the floor next to me, put his arm around me, and said, "It's going to be okay."

At the lowest moment of my life, I came face-to-face with my real self. And I came face-to-face with the truest friend.

I found him true because at that moment I had the least to offer him. I had nothing, in fact. Oh, sure, in the early days of my spiritual journey, I thought I was doing all kinds of big things for Jesus. I operated under the pretense that I was a great friend *to him*. Then all of that got torn away. I knew myself then better than I ever had. I couldn't pretend I had it all together. I couldn't fool others, and I couldn't fool myself. My true self had emerged, and he was a huge, stinking mess.

To my surprise, my friend Jesus didn't pull away. Instead, believe it or not, he got closer.

In my deepest, most despondent loneliness, I found a deeper friendship with Jesus. I learned that the power of the gospel is available even to sinful Christians who should know better.

I'm still a terrible friend to Jesus. But he is still the truest friend to me.

This spiritual reality has become the theme of my life and ministry. While I'm readily aware of the dangers of subscribing to a so-called gospel-centrality as merely an ideology or a church methodology or, even worse, a consumeristic marketing gimmick, I cannot shake the haunting of my soul of the nearness of Jesus for a sinner like me. For me, this stuff isn't a shtick. It was, and is, the difference between death and life.

This book you hold in your hands is in many ways the result of that terrible, wonderful night on that guest bedroom floor. It's also the culmination of my ensuing years of exploring friendship with Jesus not as an idea but as a daily reality. I am prone to wander. I am given to sin. But closeness with Christ has changed my life.

The possibility of friendship with Jesus is the greatest hope any soul could ever have.

It's my prayer that by reading this book you will share this hope with me. We'll begin by exploring some of the hardships of connection and the pitfalls of relationships. We'll consider some of our problems with friendships, the trouble we face having friends and being a friend. But we'll come out on the other side of that just staring into the wonder of Christ and all that he is to us and with us and for us.

If you'll let me be your friend, just for this little leg of your spiritual journey, I'll show you the Holy One who loves to make friends with sinners.

Where Did Everybody Go?

(The Possibility of Friendship with Jesus)

> Five friends I had, and two of them snakes.
>
> Frederick Buechner, *Godric*[1]

There is no friend truer than Jesus. This is a truth often difficult to believe, however, even for Christians, since we cannot see him. It's hard to believe someone is there when we cannot see them there, much less believe that this someone we cannot see is the best friend available to us. And yet this is the calling of every Christian in this age—to place faith over sight and not just trust Jesus is there but that even his invisible self is better than all the visible alternatives.

When I was a young man, it was very common to hear in church circles that Christianity is not about religion but relationship. The claim was made enough to quickly earn its place in the category of cliché. We have since found very good reasons to emphasize that Christianity is indeed "about religion," at least insofar as we have come to reap the bitter harvest of several generations lacking discipleship, spiritual formation, and emphasis on spiritual disciplines.

It turned out that what many people meant when they said "relationship not religion" was actually just a sentimental religion. And the evangelical church, particularly in the West, now suffers from this sentimental religion and all that comes with it—the treating of church like an entertainment complex, Christianity like a consumer product, and Jesus like the glorified chaplain of our self-interests. Evangelicals' relationship with Jesus is now like a Facebook friendship. We "like" him.

Biblically speaking, of course, Christianity is both religion *and* relationship. In fact, these categories, properly understood, are not so distinguishable from each other, and it turns out each must fuel the other. A relationship with Jesus without a commitment to his commands, to his church and her ordinances, to his shaping of our entire lives through the (even imperfect) pursuit of disciplines according to his likeness isn't the kind of relationship he desires from us. Similarly, a Christian religion without a spiritual hunger for his grace, a humble surrender to his character, and a desperate desire for intimacy with his very presence is just religiosity.

There's no better religion than Christianity, sure. But there is no higher, deeper, or truer human experience than to know Jesus Christ.

The most frightening portion of Scripture, to me, is undoubtedly Matthew 7:21–23, in which Jesus himself tells us that in the end, many will stand before him and claim to have done great works in his name. They will attest to miracles, prophecies, exorcisms—all under the pretense of allegiance to Jesus. And he will say to them, essentially, "I have no idea who you are."

"I never knew you," he'll say. "Depart from me" (v. 23).

I don't know about you, but I've never performed a miracle or cast out a demon. I haven't really even prophesied—at least, not in any dramatic sense of foretelling. What I have done in Jesus's name is a lot more ordinary. I've gone to church all my life, even pastored in a few. I've shared the gospel with some unbelievers here and there, though not as much as I should've. I give regularly to my church, and I give to a number of other charities besides. Generally speaking, I try to be a good person. I look out for my neighbors, I do my best to be kind to everyone, I don't (often) lie. I don't look at porn, and I don't cheat on my taxes. I vote according to Christian values. As a further advantage, I suppose, I should add that I even write Christian books and preach Christian sermons and teach at a Christian seminary.

This may all sound like bragging to you—it stands out to me right away how many sentences in the above paragraph begin with *I*—but my point is that none of these things even comes close to the kind of extravagant works Jesus declares may be performed by people he will nevertheless send to hell on the last day.

Maybe "Christianity is not a religion but a relationship" isn't too far off the mark. The sobering conclusion we must make in reading warning passages like Matthew 7:21–23 is this: you and I must take care that we *actually know Jesus*. There's no more dangerous enemy to have than Jesus. But there is also no truer friend.

Antisocial Media

A couple of years ago, when for the umpteenth time I was the subject of an online character assassination attempt, I got curious about the content of one particular hitman's social media post about me. Seeing my name tagged, I clicked on over. I wasn't shocked to see that what he'd posted was untrue. But I was shocked to see that someone I'd considered a friend had "liked" the post.

Now, I know in the grand scheme of things, people liking and unliking things on social media is the smallest potatoes you can find. I sometimes laugh when I think about the Puritans or the Reformers looking down from heaven at our obsession with social media tomfoolery. I'm sure they would find it stupid and petty and incredibly immature. But in this day and age, when we signal this way, we aren't doing something wholly insignificant. We're showing our approval, our allegiance, our alignment. So when I saw that this friend had approved a rather outrageous lie about me, it wasn't just the "like" that irritated me. It was the idea that he approved of the outrageous lie without doing what a friend ought to do in such instances—if not defend me, at the very least ask me about it.

In his defense, I suppose I should mention that we weren't extraordinarily close. But we had ministered in the same area for several years, shared meals and other fellowship, and regularly communicated in friendly and supportive ways. I certainly didn't think that if he was going through a rough time in his life I'd be high on his list of phone calls for advice, but in no way did I expect he saw me as anything less than a friend. So I messaged him.

I told him I was hurt by his endorsement of someone's un-Christlike comments about me. I acknowledged that he and I didn't see everything the same way but reaffirmed that I had considered him a friend. I also said I wished he'd brought to me personally any concerns he might have about my character.

At this point, a friend would say, "You're right. I'm sorry." Maybe they'd offer some explanation as to their reasoning that might mitigate the offense. I don't know. Instead, he said he didn't know what I was talking about, which hurt more. Either he was lying, or my reputation and character meant so little to him he couldn't even be bothered to keep track of what insults he was approving.

So I sent him a screenshot of the post, which, of course, jogged his memory. And then—get this—he asked if the accusation was true.

I paused for a moment and thought about his question, which answered my own question about how little my character meant to him. Here's what a friend would do: if he saw an accusation against me, and he wasn't sure if it was true, he would at the very least not endorse it! But ideally, he'd also reach out and ask me about it. And that's when I learned a guy I thought was a friend wasn't.

This scenario has happened to me more than once over the last few years, with some folks I've been a lot closer to than I was with this guy. This hurt was very minor compared to other friends lost, even one or two friends who effectively became enemies. Maybe you haven't experienced this particular modern form of "unfriending," but I'm willing to bet you've lost friends over the years—or people you *thought* were friends. The closer you thought them to be, the more hurt you felt.

Complicating our experience of friendship is the fact that the concept of friendship itself has become deformed in the twenty-first century. Things have been trending this way for years.

I'm not a sociologist, but I am reasonably sure that everything from the post-WWII rise of commuter culture to even the slowly changing trends in modern home architecture have contributed to an increasing sense of insulation and isolation. In his landmark 2000 book *Bowling Alone: The Collapse and Revival of American Community*, Robert Putnam expanded on an essay he published in 1995 about the deterioration of the experience of community in many of our social institutions. Clubs, civic organizations, and other "fraternal" spaces have been hemorrhaging members since the 1960s. The title of Putnam's book comes from the paradox of an increase of bowlers concurrent with the decrease in the number of bowling leagues over the years. (People are more and more likely to bowl alone.)

Your grandfather might have been a member of the Kiwanis or the Rotary or some other fraternal organization. Your father probably was not. Men my age are usually not. We have enjoyed a rise in third places—think coffee shops— where we can go to be together, and some of us do use these spaces that way, but more often than not, they are filled with people who are alone with their laptops or phones.

The smartphone, in particular, has had one of the single most detrimental effects on our experience of friendship. The first smartphone supposedly went on the market in 1994, but it was the 2007 debut of the iPhone (and its ensuing rivals) that really has done a number on us. On two fronts, the smartphone has stealthily waged a war against the necessary ingredients for the experience of friendship. First, its 24/7 access to information inflates our sense of self-sufficiency. For instance, there was a time when, if you couldn't think of the name of that supporting actor in that one movie you saw that one time, you just went on not knowing. Maybe you remembered later. But *not knowing things*, generally, was just part of life. Oh, maybe if you wondered how many miles it is from here to the moon, you could go to the library and find the answer in a book. Sometimes you could even call the information desk at the library and they would look it up for you. But more often than not, we were just used to not knowing everything. The smartphone "fixed" all that. Now everybody knows everything—or at least thinks they do. We all have instant access all the time to any bit of information we want.

Now, having ready access to all the information in the world isn't a bad thing in and of itself. But it has changed us, and not necessarily for the better. This constant access has made us less dependent on other people, more distracted from life offline (because we find it inefficient), and generally more "in our own heads." Thanks also to the internet, a lot of us don't even need to experience the social environments of workplaces, or at least not in the same way we used to.

Second, the morphing of the smartphone from luxury resource to basic utility has fundamentally changed the way we think about and interact with other people. We're "smarter" than we've ever been but are less literate. We are more "social" than we've ever been but are less socially adept. Perhaps you know that the genesis of Facebook took place in Mark Zuckerburg's Harvard dorm room as a crude online experiment comparing the relative "hotness" of female students. It eventually became a place for college students to demonstrate the relative hotness of their social lives.

Over the last decade, Facebook has become the social media platform of choice for aging baby boomers. It used to be that you had to have an .edu email domain to even get an account; now I don't know many college students who would even think about using the platform. But I also don't know many people who would argue that the aging demographic of Facebook's users has had any significant effect on the maturity of how it's used. Yes, a lot of our aunts and grandmas use it to see family photos and reconnect with high school classmates. A lot of churches use it to flexibly disseminate information to their older members. But by and large, Facebook is still a place of objectification and social dysfunction. It just revolves more around politics than collegiate interests now.

What the entirety of social media has done is provide a platform for our performative interests. We can certainly use it to communicate with friends and even to make meaningful connections with strangers, but the individualistic nature of the whole thing has proven a black hole for mature socialization. Everything we know or pretend to know must now be cut up into digestible soundbites, "hot takes," or denunciations of people and things we don't like. It honestly ought to be called *anti*social media. What was ostensibly designed to bring people together has done the opposite. We're more tempted to see others as rivals or enemies. We dehumanize and objectify, because it's easy to do that when you don't have to look someone in the face or have them look into yours.

But even when we do, it's getting harder and harder to really see people, to listen to them, to connect in substantive ways, and to interact with humility and gentleness, because the all-day pervasiveness of social media is shaping us into the kinds of people who don't want to.

I don't know if you're buying any of this, but if you are, you can probably also see how, for Christians, the shaping influence of social media culture poses a real danger of making us act less like Jesus. And the less we become like Jesus, the less we will understand how to do real friendship.

Putting the *I* in Friend

There are other significant factors in the deformation of relationships, of course. One huge influence on the rise of dehumanization and objectification in our day has been the rise of porn addiction across multiple generations. We could also mention other contributors such as our modern cultural sacraments of workaholism and busyness and expressive individualism. The latter is an especially growing threat and making sizable inroads within evangelicalism.

It turns out that, because of the fall detailed in Genesis 3, none of us needs help in becoming self-interested, self-centered people, but we have endless innovations at our disposal to aid an increasing focus on self-exaltation. We've even smuggled this self-focus, in the form of consumerism, into our experience of spirituality.

What do you get when thirty years of attractional church programming—which is oriented largely around consumer tastes and individual "application"—meets a secular philosophy oriented around the god of the self, in which *the* truth is subservient to "my truth" and questions of identity are answered not in traditional religion but in cultural expressions of race, politics, and sexuality? Well, the nuanced answer is that you get tribalism instead of true community.

Tribes aren't all bad, of course. We all have a tribe or two. Tribes, plainly put, are where we share mutual interests and affinities. The problem with a lot of modern tribalism, however, is that it provides an illusion of belonging founded largely on a mutual grievance or self-interest. And a bunch of people together all focused on themselves isn't usually a place where self-sacrificial relationships germinate.

We see this in the increasing fundamentalist spirit of tribes both on the extreme left and extreme right of politics. If you're familiar with the horseshoe theory, you know what I'm talking about. It basically goes like this: the further to the extreme left or right one's views go, the closer they get to the extreme of the other side. Which is why we now face the increase of angry authoritarianism threatening us from opposite sides of the political aisle. Extreme leftists and rightists both want to ban books and qualify free speech. Both want to curtail (different aspects of) religious liberty. Both are in favor of (different kinds of) authoritarian government. And both have given rise to instances of political violence.

This extreme tribalism, following two generations of entertainment-driven faith, is now more and more deforming the growth of honest faith in Christian churches. It becomes difficult to open up to anybody, to share one's fears or hurts or sins, to "do life" together when you know you're just one misstep away from being declared an enemy by someone who claimed to be your brother or sister. Extreme tribalism on the right has made it more costly for some Christians to talk about their experiences of racism or injustice and made any Christian questioning of the moral character of Republican politicians into a kind of heresy. Extreme tribalism on the left has made it more costly for some Christians to simply affirm what the Bible says about gender and sexuality, things Christians have affirmed largely without internal controversy for two thousand years, and has turned every Bible story into a case study on identity politics or critical theory.

Extreme tribalism can even distort how we hear God's voice. When tales of royal victory in the Old Testament are taken out of context and thrust onto modern American patriotism, or when the closeness between David and Jonathan is twisted to sanction homosexuality, we are hearing what theologian Carl Trueman calls "the triumph of the modern self"[2] over the clear voice of the Spirit.

So now that we all suspect each other, now that we all have our own interests at heart, now that most of our interactions and opinions are tuned toward the performative and the belligerent, how is it exactly any of us are supposed to know what real friendship is like?

Friendship Made for Trouble

We're in a big mess. Thankfully, many of us nevertheless are journeying through this cultural morass of social deformation with a few friends. But I'll tell you, one of the hardest parts of navigating these recent days—one of the hardest parts of just getting older, actually—is finding out who your friends *aren't*.

This is one of the key truths I've learned about friendship in the last ten years: a friend isn't someone who's close when it's enjoyable to be close but one who doesn't bail when it's not. They may not always stand right by your side when everything goes sideways in your life, but they're not running away either. At the very least, they're certainly not helping things go sideways! And the best friends are the ones who not only stay by your side but aim to help you face what you're facing.

Proverbs 17:17 says, "A friend loves at all times, and a brother is born for adversity" (ESV). I like that, in part, because of what it doesn't say. It doesn't say a brother is born *from* adversity. It's kind of rare to make true friends in the midst of difficult times. Sometimes it works. I think of soldiers who come home as brothers for life because of the shared and profound experience of war. It's hard to break a bond born of holding someone else's life in your hands. Similarly, there's a bond that sometimes develops between someone who needed rescuing from a deadly situation and the one who courageously rescued them. But mostly, we make friends in ordinary times of social interaction—at work, at school, at church, at the park, on a team, and so forth. We have some things in common we can talk about. We have mutual interests we can share. We do things together and share secrets and share jokes and share dreams.

Then trouble comes. And you find out if all of it added up to friendship or not. A real friend loves at all times, and a brother is born *for* the adversity.

As hard as it is sometimes to face, it's the winnowing of friends through various adversities that helps us love our remaining friends more. On the one hand, I'm afraid to admit that in my late forties, I have fewer close friends than I did when I was in my early twenties. It's especially sobering given the current deadly epidemic of loneliness among middle-aged men. But on the other hand, I'm happy to know that the few friends I've got left have pretty much seen it all! They've been through the fire with me and have emerged showing their trueness. These are the guys with whom I'd walk into more adversity.

I think of that moment in the movie *Tombstone* when, after narrowly surviving a nasty gunfight together, a member of Wyatt Earp's outfit asks the sickly, frail Doc Holliday why he'd leave his bed to risk his life in such a dangerous way.

Holliday simply says, "Wyatt Earp is my friend."

His questioner responds, "Hell, I got lots of friends," to which Holliday replies, "Well, I don't."[3]

Once upon a time, I was leading a young adult ministry at a very large church, and I believed God was calling me to break away and plant that ministry as an independent church of our own. I didn't want to be divisive, and I met with our host church's leaders to explain my vision. They understood and, amazingly, gave their blessing. But I knew I had a leadership team for the young adult ministry that was too large for a small church plant. I also knew that some of those leaders, ones previously recruited by the first organizer of our ministry, had never really shared my particular vision for teaching and mission. I knew a division was on the horizon. We had a difficult meeting where I basically laid out the intended plan. There was pushback. There was confusion. A line was being drawn. It didn't get heated. Nobody seemed angry. But a severe disappointment settled into the room.

In a way it was clarifying. For all of us. And in the end, that leadership team essentially split. Just four leaders felt called to leave and help plant a new church with me. And while I was nervous about losing some talented folks in key areas of ministry that would be hugely helpful in starting a new work, the five of us remaining leaders became even closer.

It's not easy to plant a church. We were trying to do something none of us had done before and something not many were yet doing in our context—plant a gospel-centered, missional church. But being "in the trenches" together made us closer. It created a joy in our work, even as we struggled to grow a tiny ministry, that I am incredibly thankful for to this day.

That church plant doesn't exist anymore. But our friendships do. In fact, nearly twenty years later, two of those leaders are still two of the best friends my wife and I have.

Real friendships endure.

Real friendships are made for trouble. Because how can you know? How can you know if someone is a true friend if you experience only agreement and happiness and comfort together? Just like our marriage vows are only as true as our experience together of the sickness and poverty and death doing us part. It's easy to be married when marriage is easy. And it's easy to be friends when friendship is easy.

And all of this brings me back to the concept of friendship with Jesus. Because he sees a lot more than even my closest friends do. He doesn't just see the things I tweet or post; he sees the things I think, the things I desire. I don't pretend to be a trouble-free person, but even my wife doesn't know the half of it. Yet Jesus sees it all. So I think of Matthew 7:23 and shudder.

What a Friend We Have in Jesus

It's somewhat encouraging to me to know Jesus himself experienced abandonment by his friends. And then I think about the fact that I still abandon him just about every day in little circumstances here and there. That's not so encouraging. In fact, I'm pretty terrible at friendship myself. But if anything, my regular awareness of my awfulness makes me tune in even closer to his responses to these kinds of momentary betrayals.

The truth is, we're all terrible friends to Jesus. But he is still the truest friend we could have. In John 15:15, Jesus says to his disciples, "I do not call you servants anymore, because a servant doesn't know what his master is doing. I have called you friends, because I have made known to you everything I have heard from my Father."

He calls his disciples *friends*. He says this before his arrest, before his crucifixion, before the sorrowful disappointment of his burial, knowing full well his friends are about to fail him. He knows they're going to betray him, abandon him, and deny him. And he still calls them friends.

Contrasted with what he promises in Matthew 7:23 to say to people who claimed to do all kinds of awesome things for him, we must wonder, *What gives?*

Let's just consider the scene of his arrest, for instance (Mark 14:43–50). Jesus and his disciples have just eaten the Passover meal, during which they enjoyed an incredibly intimate fellowship, reclining against each other at the table. Jesus is preparing them for his death and what will come after. These are precious moments building one on top of another, the commitment of Christ to his followers—and they to him—in stark relief.

31

Now they have retired to the garden of Gethsemane, where Jesus intercedes in prayer for them. Thus begins the narrative downhill slope to the base of the mount of Calvary. While he's been praying in agony, his friends have been sleeping, so he wakes them up and alerts them that his betrayal and arrest are imminent.

The pace of the scene in Mark's Gospel is almost breathless. Mark goes toward the cross at a breakneck pace, rushing even more quickly at this point than before. Each of the episodes leading up to the crucifixion is short and punchy. You can feel the dizzying hurry of it all. And this feeling is captured especially in the arrest scene. It almost feels like chaos once things get rolling.

But Jesus stands out in this scene by contrast to all of the panic swirling around him. Do you remember that time in a boat where everyone was freaking out while Jesus was sleeping? Well, now as the real storm approaches, Jesus in the garden is the only one awake while everyone else is taking a nap. But after the disciples have been roused, they go right back into panic mode. Jesus alone projects a kind of stillness.

This little scene is important, because it shows us yet again the stark contrast between Jesus and ourselves. So often our desires, our passions, and our sacrifices don't have Jesus at the center of them as supremely worthy.

Judas's actions are the most obvious example here. This man's priorities haven't been subtle! He's practically been telegraphing this moment for days. Jesus predicted this was going to happen, but Judas, as far as we know, spent no time demurring or denying. Unlike with Peter's foretold denial, there's no parallel scene of Judas saying, "I would never do that!"

The betrayer thinks he can play it cool. But we know that his desire is about money and control. In Mark 14:11, we're told the promise of money set up Judas's desire to betray his Lord. And that fatal trajectory culminates here. In verse 45, he greets Jesus with the honorific of "Rabbi," which is the customary sign of a disciple to his master. But it's only a ruse. It's a falsely expressed desire. It's all a lie.

Judas does this, we're told elsewhere, for just thirty pieces of silver, which isn't all that much money. I mean, it's not exactly chump change, but it's not a fortune either. In today's dollars, depending on what kind of silver coins were paid, it'd be somewhere between one hundred and four hundred dollars. Certainly not nearly enough, you would think, to trade in for allegiance to the true King of Israel.

But when your desires are disordered, you'll see worth in unworthy places. When your desires are disordered, you'll hold cheap things as costly and costly things as cheap.

I wonder if Jesus was even communicating this truth in a subtle, ironic way. Knowing Judas was a greedy betrayer right out of the gate, he still put Judas in charge of the money (John 12:6)! Why would he do that? I don't know, except perhaps to show us that Jesus holds money loosely. Maybe it's also meant to show us that *we* ought to as well. And while Jesus isn't endorsing greed, of course, he has orchestrated this entire thing as the Lord of the universe to bring to the surface how even our greatest earthly treasures are a mere pittance compared to his own all-surpassing glory.

There are so many biblical scenes that point to this truth. There's the parable about the man who sold everything he had in order to get the field where the treasure was buried, and the parable about the man who sold everything he had in order to get that one priceless pearl. But the most heartbreaking scenes are probably the ones where someone *doesn't* see the surpassing worth of Christ and his kingdom. In Mark 10, for example, Jesus meets the man we know as the rich young ruler. "Sell all you have," Jesus basically tells him. "Give it to the poor. And then come follow me." Jesus wants this young man to trade his great treasure for the greater, far-surpassing treasure of Jesus himself. But verse 22 tells us the young man went away dismayed and grieving. His desire was disordered. In the very next scene, Jesus tells his disciples, "How hard it is for those who have wealth to enter the kingdom of God!" (10:23).

It's a startling pronouncement. And we should apply it well. You may not have a lot of money, but where is your wealth? Do you treasure it more than Jesus?

Judas's desires weren't ordered around Jesus. Ultimately, money was his god. Money may not be your god of choice, but the point still applies to us. Our desires reveal our true object of worship. What are you tempted to pursue, what do you crave, what do you long for *more* than the friendship of your Savior? Only he can satisfy. Only he can deliver on all his promises. Only he can give us true joy.

But perhaps Judas's example isn't the most apt for our particular lack of commitment to Jesus. Very few of us would betray our Savior, right? At least, not that way. But what about betrayals of a different kind?

"One of those who stood by drew his sword, struck the high priest's servant, and cut off his ear" (Mark 14:47). We know from the account in John's Gospel that the servant's name is Malchus and the impulsive swordsman is Peter. Now, we already know Peter is a pretty passionate guy. He speaks when he shouldn't. He's constantly jockeying for position. He jumps out of boats. He even tries to rebuke Jesus at times.

Here Peter's passion gets the best of him again. But what is really driving this passion? Protecting Jesus? Maybe. More immediately, however, we may think of Peter's actions as being driven by a persistent worldly conception about the kingdom of God.

See, Peter's vision, not unlike that of most Jews of his time, is that the Messiah's coming must involve a violent, political overthrow of the Roman oppressors. Most of the messianic expectation in this day revolved around images of warfare, of physical liberation, of punishing their foreign occupiers.

On the surface, it may seem like Peter is doing a good thing, a sincere thing, defending Jesus. But it's really his own self-centered agenda at work, his own ambition, his own misunderstanding and misuse of the notion of the kingdom of God.

I don't think I'm making this up. In Matthew's parallel account, we even see that Jesus rebuked Peter for this very notion, saying after this violent outburst, "Put your sword back in its place because all who take up the sword will perish by the sword" (26:52). And in Luke's account we know that Jesus then goes on to pick up Malchus's ear and stick it back on its bloody stump (22:51). In other words, Jesus is saying, "Peter, my kingdom doesn't come by worldly passions. It doesn't come by violent overthrow of our earthly enemies. It comes by laying down our lives."

Doing worldly things in Jesus's name isn't the same as treasuring Jesus. And as that scary passage in Matthew 7 warns us, even doing *religious* things in Jesus's name isn't always the same as treasuring Jesus.

There are a lot of people claiming to speak for God today, a lot of people claiming to do things in Jesus's name. Every day on social media we find professing Christians cursing their enemies, reviling their brothers and sisters, hating each other—all somehow in the name of Jesus.

Is it possible that our chopping off ears in Jesus's name is no different from a betrayer's kiss? It has the appearance of affection, the appearance of passion, but it has self at the center.

When the children of Israel made that golden calf in the wilderness and began to worship it, Exodus 32:5 tells us that Aaron ascribed their worship to God! They made an idol to worship but somehow also made the claim that they weren't trading in their allegiance to YHWH. They were bowing to the golden calf and calling it worship of the Lord.

But what would it look like to see Jesus as worthy of our greatest passion? It would look exactly as he said—through self-crucifixion, it would look like loving our enemies, blessing those who persecute us, and being willing to be counted among the rubbish of this world if it means aligning with the way of Christ. It means handing our lives as a blank check over to the true Lord, surrendering our passions to him to channel as he pleases. It means repenting of our ways and going his, no matter the cost. It means seeing him as so, so worthy of our greatest passion.

Jesus Stands Alone

In the end, when all of these would-be followers of Jesus in Mark 14 realize their own ways are crumbling, the crisis proves devastating to them. They don't see friendship with Jesus as worth the incredible cost. He has told them that following him means "[taking] up their cross" (Matt. 16:24), but when it comes time to do it, Jesus is left to the cross alone.

Mark 14:50 is haunting: "They all deserted him and ran away." In that moment, there were more precious things to all of them than Jesus. He wasn't worthy of their greatest passion.

Jesus calls all of his disciples to lay down their lives for his sake. This includes you and me, if we consider ourselves followers of Jesus. It's worth looking into the future from Mark 14 a bit to be reminded that tradition tells us Peter, the impetuous idolater in this scene and the ardent denier of Jesus in the next scene (vv. 66–72), goes on after his restoration to a great apostolic ministry and even to his own death on a cross, which he requested be executed upside down. Why? Because he didn't consider himself worthy even of Christ's death. Somehow Peter found the grace to find Christ worthy of the greatest sacrifice.

And Jesus is certainly worthy of our sacrifice. But ours isn't the greatest. The apostle Peter's upside-down crucifixion, as terrifying and terrible as that was, wasn't the greatest sacrifice either. No, Christ's sacrifice is the greatest. And ultimately, Christ had to go to the cross because he alone is holy. He alone is sinless. He alone could make sufficient atonement for idolaters like Peter and idolaters like you and me. He alone is a true friend.

Only Jesus is worthy of the greatest sacrifice. Only Jesus is worthy enough for the cross.

Ultimately, the reason Jesus made the greatest sacrifice is not because we're worthy of it but because he is. His glory is the greatest reality in all of existence. His name is above every name. His holiness prevails over all.

The rebellion of sinners cannot—and will not—have the final word, the final say, the final victory. Mark 14:49 is in fact an exclamation point on this truth: "The Scriptures must be fulfilled."

At the cross, Jesus wins the ultimate victory, because he alone is worthy. And we will be singing for all eternity, according to Revelation 5:12, not "We are worthy," but "Worthy is the Lamb who was slaughtered!" Worthy is *he* "to receive power and riches and wisdom and strength and honor and glory and blessing!" Forever and ever, amen!

And while this makes so much of God and so little of us, it is still such good news for us. In fact, it couldn't be good news for us if it weren't true. You and I aren't worthy of that sacrifice, not worthy of that cross.

If even the most religious or most moral person we could find died on that cross for us, we'd still be dead in our sins, because even the best person is still a sinner. Only Jesus could make the atoning sacrifice for us, because only Jesus is a sinless Savior. Only Jesus could be a spotless sacrifice. Only Jesus is good enough to make the sacrifice that satisfies the just wrath of God. And it's only in Jesus, then, that we find the worthiness to enter the glorious presence of our holy God.

It's only through Jesus that we can even be friends with Jesus. His blood purchases our passage into his everlasting life.

Isaiah 53:6 says that all of us like sheep have gone astray. All of us, born sinners, have deserted God and run away. In the garden, at the cross, out of the tomb, at the right hand of the Father, Christ stands alone as a true friend. He alone is worthy of the greatest sacrifice. And yet—and yet!—with this same great sacrifice, he welcomes sinners like you and me back into his worthiness. He is willing to be treated like us—like a criminal (Mark 14:48)—that we criminals might be treated like him.

You know, this isn't the first time the holiness of God ran people out of a garden. In this garden of Gethsemane we see everybody running for their lives, including apparently some young guy who leaves his nightgown to flee the garden naked (vv. 51–52). Back in the garden of Eden, fresh from the fall, having chosen some other treasure over their Lord, Adam and Eve were naked and ashamed, vulnerable. Deserving of the wrath of a holy God. And they were exiled from Eden, sent fleeing from the garden.

But just as the Lord covered Adam and Eve's shame with the skins of sacrifices (Gen. 3:21), he can cover ours with the greater sacrifice of himself.

Our garment of shame becomes Christ's, who bears our shame for us. And Christ's garment of spotless white becomes ours, as our shame has been covered by his righteousness. He does this for all of his lousy friends. Even for Peter the denier.

This is the kind of friend Jesus is. There is none truer. No friend was born for adversity like him. Despite our petty compromises, despite our misplaced passions, despite our frequent lapses into idolatry and our constant trading in of our commitment to him for interest in a million different things nowhere close to worthy of his name, he doesn't call us servants. He calls us *friends*.

What do you suppose we should do with information like that?

Servants or Friends?

(The Reality of Friendship with Jesus)

I see my Saviour where I looked for hay.

C. S. Lewis, "The Nativity"[1]

There is no friend so real as Jesus. There's never been anyone so self-assured, so secure, so socially un-awkward as Jesus. He never puts on airs. He never has to fake it till he makes it. He never pretends to be anything other than who he really is. Jesus is the realest deal going—in the first-century world of social unrest, spiritual one-upmanship, and religious fakery and in our modern world of the same.

Recently, a candidate for political office quipped from her campaign stage that if Jesus had an assault rifle, he'd "still be alive today." It was a short sentence expressing a simple assertion, and it revealed a hundred wrong things about Jesus. But if I had to boil down the wrongness to near its essence, I might say it like this: there are people out there who want to use Jesus for their own ends, and they don't see that not actually knowing him is a liability. You can't use him for your own ends even if you *do* know him.

Jesus will not be used. But he will be known.

Or at least he *can* be. Which in itself is quite staggering. If we'd ever get around to stop trying to use him, we'd be in constant awe that the Son of God condescends to be known by losers like us.

When you take all of the problems outlined previously and pile them up into the human experience, the disadvantage is practically insurmountable. More and more, we don't know how to "do friendship." We're losing our ability to relate to each other in open and authentic ways. It's getting harder to have conversations that aren't in some way performative or otherwise self-interested. We feel more beholden to our grievances than to our neighbors. The polarizing pull of our tribal identity is stronger than our need to be known. And then underneath and on top of all of that is just the basic biblical fact that we're sinners who by nature fall short of the glory of God, and the prospect of communing with this invisible God seems laughable.

Even when people use language like "feeling God's presence" or "experiencing God," they're usually talking about things they can hear and see and touch, such as listening to music or walking through the woods. The idea that any of us weirdos could just sit down—anywhere!—and have a conversation with the God of the universe sounds too, well, "out there."

41

When I was a teenager, I once went on a retreat with my church youth group into the Sandia Mountains outside of Albuquerque, New Mexico. One sunny morning we were sent out individually into the wilderness and told not to return until we had heard from God. The prospect was thrilling. The wilderness is where God meets people! And I loved the idea of giving God a whole day to speak to me.

We weren't given any specific instructions about how to hear from God. This was before cell phones, so they didn't even need to tell us to leave our phones in the cabin. They just sent us out with our own hearts and minds.

I didn't hear anything. I sat out in a shady spot on a big rock, tracing the toes of my sneakers in the dirt, slapping bugs that landed on my arms and flinching every time I heard a rustle in the bushes, sure I'd see a bear, and listened for a voice that never came.

That evening, when we gathered in the cabin to recount the spiritual exploits of the day, I made something up about what God had said to me. I don't remember what it was. But I didn't want to be the only one God didn't speak to, and everybody else had a story to tell. I don't want to call them liars, but I think they were liars. We all were. All, that is, but one of us. One young woman, through tears, confessed she hadn't heard anything. She wondered what was wrong with her. She asked why God spoke to everybody else but not to her.

I wasn't old enough then to understand the spiritual dynamics of what was taking place, but now I recognize we all did her a kind of harm. Because we faked some direct hotline to heaven, our one honest friend felt shame and condemnation. But in telling the truth, she was the strongest one in the circle. We were all drunk on the idea that we could just go out and have a conversation with Jesus.

Can I tell you something? Despite the idiot spirituality of that youth retreat, I still believe we can.

Talking with God isn't truly a matter of feeling our way through anything. It's not about listening to shifts in the wind or creaking in the trees. It's not about putting out a fleece. And it's definitely not about looking for signs in the clouds or for faces in burnt toast. It's much more mystical than that—but also a lot more real.

Here is one of the most thrilling verses of Scripture: "The LORD would speak with Moses face to face, just as a man speaks with his friend" (Exod. 33:11). My mind goes back to this verse over and over again, several times a week, and when it does my heart wants to leap out of my chest. I think, *I want that.*

In Genesis 3, we read that Adam and Eve hear the Lord walking in the garden in the cool of the evening. In this particular instance, he's coming to bring judgment on their disobedience, but I don't think they're unfamiliar with the sound of the Lord's footsteps in their home.

Some will say, "But that's the Old Testament. There are a lot of things in the Old Testament that people experienced that are not normative for us." No doubt. Pillars of fire and smoke, parted seas, bodily rapture into heaven à la Enoch and Elijah. But regardless of epochs or dispensations, there's a constant for God's people: we have a God who wants to be known.

I don't know what it means for Moses to see God face-to-face or for God to walk in the garden of Eden. Are these metaphors for God's palpable nearness? Are they Christophanies, preincarnate physical appearances of the Son of God? I'll let the theologians hypothesize. Whether these unique experiences continue or not, I can't authoritatively say, but I do know that God still draws near, that he still speaks, and that we can, believe it or not, *be friends with him*.

The reality of friendship with Jesus, though, depends on a serious reckoning with the reality of Jesus. Most of us, Christians included, have grown accustomed to conducting a relationship with *the idea* of Jesus. But Jesus is a real person. The fact that we cannot see him does not negate this fact. The fact that we cannot see him doesn't even mean that he cannot be seen!

Real Christianity affirms a real resurrection, in which the real Jesus really rose from being really dead into a glorious new real life. I'll say a bit more about this later, but it wasn't a ghost that came back from the grave. The resurrected Jesus wasn't real merely "in the hearts" of his disciples. He was really in front of their faces. And when he ascended into heaven, he ascended in his real body, which is now somehow taking up tangible space in the hyperspatial dimension where God's manifest presence is fully realized.

Jesus has a face with eyes and a nose and all the other stuff that, you know, a face generally has. He has arms and legs. He has a real body. He is the Son of God, yes, and the Son is also omnipresent and omniscient. But he's also eternally incarnate, though now risen and transformed. He is in fact filling all things (Eph. 4:10), and this will someday include our very vision. We can't see him now, but someday (soon) we will (1 Cor. 13:12). He can be seen; thus, he can be known.

When we relate to Jesus as an idea rather than as a real person, we might make our discipleship feel more efficient and productive, somehow more tangible and more "real," but we're short-circuiting the deep heart work Christ's Spirit is dedicated to performing in us. I'll say more about this practice in chapter 5, but for now, let me introduce the idea this way: "wasting time" with *the person* of Jesus is far more impactful in all the ways that eternally matter than "getting things done" with the idea of him is. Therefore, relating to Jesus as a real person has implications for our understanding of personal spiritual disciplines and our communion with God.

Servant Spirituality versus Friendship Spirituality

Taking another look at John 15:15, I think we can see a Christ-directed premise for our communion with him: "I do not call you servants anymore. . . . I have called you friends."

Teasing this out can be a little tricky, because in one sense we're very much still to be servants of Christ. The apostles very often utilized servant language to characterize their relationship with their Lord. Paul, Peter, and James all refer to themselves as servants of the Lord. The Greek word here is *doulos*, which is more directly translated "bondservant" and more literally means "slave." The apostles refer to themselves as essentially "slaves of Christ."

Further, the very concepts of Jesus as Lord and as King—among other biblical titles—presuppose a master-servant relationship. For that matter, the reality that Jesus is fully God presupposes a master-servant dynamic!

So I'm not about to argue that "servant" is an inappropriate, much less unbiblical, referent for our relationship with Jesus. But when we dig deeper into the spiritual dynamic giving rise to this language, I think we can see a little bit of a twist not often considered. For the apostles, as for ourselves, to reckon ourselves slaves or servants of Jesus isn't exactly to typify our relationship with him (e.g., like a slave would relate to a master) but rather our status before him (e.g., like a slave is bound to a master). Indeed, we're told that Christians aren't given a "spirit of slavery" (Rom. 8:15) in relation to God but a spirit more akin to adoption. In other words, by referring to themselves as "slaves" and "servants," I don't believe the apostles are saying that God treats us like slaves but that we nonetheless belong body and soul to God alone.

I think, in a way, Jesus is getting at this distinction in John 15:15. For instance, he says that a "servant doesn't know what his master is doing." He calls us friends, because he has "made known to [us] everything [he has] heard from [his] Father."

One directive from owning our status as bondservants of Christ is remembering the holy *otherness* of God. Servants remember to be reverent in their communion with God, not flippant. They remember to "hallow" God's name (Matt. 6:9 ESV).

And yet servants don't have full and open access to their masters. They don't operate from a baseline of favor and freedom with their masters. They aren't let into the inner life and eternal plans of their masters. But friends experience all of these things. This is why I want to argue that our Christian faith, while anchored in our status as servants of Christ our King, is felt as real and transformative in our relationship as intimates of Christ our friend.

Consider the spiritual pursuits of two hypothetical believers. I'll call them Christian S. and Christian F.

Christian S. gets up early every morning and reads his Bible according to a daily plan that will take him through the entirety of the Scriptures in a year. He prays the written prayer at the end of his devotional, sometimes adding specific requests for himself and others he knows. Throughout the day, Christian S. listens to Christian music while he works, and during his break he peruses Christian websites. In the evening, Christian S. leads family worship for his wife and children around the dinner table. Before he goes to bed, he recites a routine prayer.

On Sundays, Christian S. loads his family up in the minivan and drives them to church. In Sunday school, he squirms a bit during share time but enjoys learning more about the Bible during the teaching. Christian S. is a bit of an armchair academic. He likes answering questions correctly and adding to his trove of Bible knowledge.

During the worship service, Christian S. just listens to the more modern songs but sings along to the older ones, mainly because they please him with their familiarity. When it's time for the preaching, he takes copious notes and frequently gets frustrated when he misses the next thing the pastor says because he was still trying to record the previous thing.

After lunch out, where Christian S. makes sure he leaves a good tip, wanting to represent the "church crowd" well, his family returns home. Christian S. notices several of his neighbors mowing their yards, and he doesn't realize he's a little chagrined. He doesn't realize that he's thinking he's better than them for having dedicated his Sunday to the Lord.

This regimen constitutes the spirituality of Christian S. He's not an unbeliever, not by any stretch. He's not a fake Christian. He's invested in this disciplined routine because he sincerely believes in God and in the gospel, and he takes God's commandments and his own pursuit of holiness seriously. But if you asked him at any given moment what it feels like to be close to God, he would look at you puzzled. "What do feelings really have to do with anything?" he'd say, not exactly understanding the question. "Facts are superior to feelings."

Indeed they are. But when other Christians come to Christian S. looking for counsel or help, they don't experience him as particularly empathetic. He strikes many around him as being deep in conviction but shallow in compassion.

Does Christian S. experience closeness to God? In a way, yes, because he commits so much time to spiritual things like Bible reading, prayer, and church services. But in another way, no, because he's treating all of these things as ends unto themselves, the mechanism by which to simply be a religious person. All of his religious efforts are generally oriented around knowing more and doing more—both good things—but this knowing and doing still fall short of the sort of being God plans to transform us into.

The Holy Spirit uses all of our efforts in the spiritual disciplines toward our good. And none of us engages in the disciplines totally free from self-interest or the corrupting influence of self-righteousness. But there's approaching the spiritual life as something to master (relating to Jesus as an idea), and there's approaching the spiritual life as something that masters us (relating to Jesus as a person).

Now, of course, reverence and discipline are good! But treating Christian spirituality like a chore chart or performance review is not. The former are important reminders that while Christ is our friend, he isn't our peer. The latter treats Christ like an idea, a reward dispenser.

Now consider Christian F. He isn't nearly as disciplined as Christian S., which is definitely not a good thing. Christian F. wakes up to his alarm but rarely feels awake until after he's had a couple of cups of coffee. He opens his Bible and reads through a booger-eyed daze. Sometimes he uses a reading plan, but more often he just opens to a book he hasn't read in a while. Christian F. is no theologian. He would lose against the average fifth grade Sunday school student in any Bible trivia contest. But he tries. He wants to know the meaning of what he's reading. So he constantly asks God, "Help me out here, Lord." Christian F. also wants to know what difference the Scripture he's reading will make in his life. He doesn't always see it, but he trusts that meaning is there and prays even more that God will show him.

When Christian F. goes to church, he feels lost quite a bit in Sunday school. A lot of it is over his head. But he does love the Bible, and he soaks in what he can. He also loves it when there's discussion, because he likes hearing from his brothers and sisters. As he hears their hurts or fears or challenges or joys or wonders or successes, he prays for them. Inwardly he mourns for them or celebrates with them, whatever the case may be.

Christian F. is sometimes a minute or two late to the service because he spends time encouraging people or asking if there are ways he can pray for them. Sometimes he lingers to ask the Sunday school teacher to explain a couple of things he didn't understand but didn't want to interrupt the flow of class to ask about.

In the worship service, Christian F., like a lot of churchgoers, likes some songs more than others, but he does his best to sing along with them all, whether he "feels" them or not, and he discovers that in all of them there's something good worth thinking about. And like a lot of churchgoers, Christian F. likes some sermons more than others, but he especially likes when the preacher gets to Jesus. This isn't because Christian F. thinks the parts of the Bible that don't mention Jesus aren't inerrant or infallible or authoritative but because he's come to suspect the whole thing is really about Jesus. And so when the preacher finally gets there, it feels like a crescendo of sorts, like they've made it to some great summit.

Christian F. is a messy prayer. He often wanders and rambles. He's reverent but not formal. He mainly talks to God as if he's talking to another person. This can make him uncomfortable when he's asked to pray aloud in group settings. He's not sure he knows how to pray with all those "Father Gods" and "Dear Lords" everybody else seems so good at adding. He's also not sure how to pray without confessing sin. Christian F. sometimes forgets to ask for things besides forgiveness; he usually spends his prayer time telling God about his day and all that went with it and then admitting all the stuff he knows he got wrong. Christian F. doesn't know how not to be himself in prayer.

Now, what's the major difference between Christian S. and Christian F.?

I know I've stacked the deck a bit with these imaginary stand-ins. And I'm honestly not trying to criticize discipline and formality while celebrating casualness and informality. I'm certainly not trying to denigrate theological knowledge. (As a seminary professor and local church pastor, that'd be a dumb thing for me to do.) But in these admitted caricatures I'm trying to highlight two different ways we often relate to God and engage in spiritual pursuits.

Christian S. represents a servant spirituality. Christian F. represents a friendship spirituality. And the honest truth is that I'm not thinking of different people when I paint these contrasting portraits; I'm thinking of myself. Day to day, season to season, I've been both Christian F. and Christian S. If you've walked with Jesus long enough, you probably have too.

I notice a distinct—dare I say *felt*—difference when I'm relating to Jesus as a real person, despite a lack of regimented disciplines. Now, the smart Christian would ask, "Why not both?" Indeed. Jesus himself says that if we really love him, we will keep his commandments (John 14:15). The real key to experiencing deep and renewing change by grace is to dedicate oneself to daily communion with Jesus, which necessarily includes a serious commitment to obedience. But his commands are not burdensome (1 John 5:3). Furthermore, I think too few locate this key because the disciplines themselves seem more manageable than the person of Jesus seems experienceable.

To move from a servant spirituality to a friendship spirituality means *really believing*—and not just theologically—that Jesus is a real person.

Jesus Is a Real Person

I very much want you to contemplate this reality. To reach a fuller possibility of friendship with Jesus and to experience spiritual newness through closeness with him depends largely on how real you believe him to be. Relating to *the idea* of Jesus can make you a smarter Christian, a nicer Christian, a more religious Christian, but it cannot make you a deeper, more joyful, or more authentically Christlike Christian.

Indeed, as the aim of spiritual growth in Christianity is to become more conformed to the image of Christ, it behooves us to remember that for Christ to be made real in us, we must be drawing near to a real Christ.

In 2 Corinthians 3:18, the apostle Paul speaks of the Christian being transformed into the likeness of Jesus, one degree at a time, through the beholding of Jesus's glory. Paul says this comes about when we look at Jesus with "an unveiled face." He's referring to a relational intimacy, a spiritual focus not simply on the edifice around Jesus—that's a servant kind of spirituality—but on the person of Jesus, on his glory. In fact, the entirety of 2 Corinthians 3 could be seen as a contrast between servant spirituality (relating to God purely through the glory of the law) and friendship spirituality (relating to God further through the glory of the Good News). Paul says the ministry of the Spirit is far more glorious than the ministry of the law (vv. 8–9).

Paul emphasizes sight here, even if only in the spiritual sense, in a way that reminds us of the see-ability of our Lord. This is a concept the apostles keep coming back to over and over again. Paul himself sees the risen Christ after the ascension, when he's hijacked on that road to Damascus, and that vision changes him. And while everything he commends in his letters is undoubtedly and irrefutably Spiritual (capital *S* intentional), this doesn't mean none of it is real or predicated on tangible truths, even if they aren't yet fully tangible for the rest of us. In a similar way, Paul stresses the tangible reality of Christ's resurrected body when exhorting the Corinthians to hope in a resurrection still invisible to them in the present time (1 Cor. 15:12–20).

In his first epistle, the apostle John refers back to the reality of Christ as a person to establish the foundation for spiritual fellowship with God:

> What was from the beginning, what we have heard, *what we have seen with our eyes, what we have observed and have touched with our hands*, concerning the word of life—that life was revealed, and we have seen it and we testify and declare to you the eternal life that was with the Father and was revealed to us—what we have seen and heard we also declare to you, so that you may also have fellowship with us; and indeed our fellowship is with the Father and with his Son, Jesus Christ. We are writing these things so that our joy may be complete. (1 John 1:1–4, emphasis added)

John knows that many of his recipients may struggle with faith and with hope, given the invisibility of the Lord they worship. (This is one reason why idolatry so naturally arises from our flesh; it's just easier to put our trust in and give ultimate authority to things we can see and feel.) So he reminds them of Christ's visibility and touchability. John has walked with Jesus. He isn't holding forth the idea of God but the very revelation of God in the flesh through the incarnation. And John is ensuring his recipients that Jesus, while ascended, is still very real. He is telling them that joy that's real comes from fellowship that's real with the Son of God who is real.

This may be difficult to believe, but it's to our advantage at this time that Jesus is invisible. Jesus himself said so (John 16:7). It's why he sent the church the Holy Spirit upon his ascension. The incarnate Christ takes up physical space. The incarnate Son cannot at this time be seen by all believers any more than he could during his earthly ministry. But the Spirit of Christ can take up residence in every believer's life. We can all enjoy fellowship with the Son because of the Spirit's manifest presence in the life of all Christ's church.

Think of that moment of crucial tangibility after the resurrection. Jesus has appeared to his disciples. His body is glorified, transformed, and yet is still him. He can somehow walk through locked doors and yet still bears the scars of crucifixion. Thomas struggles to believe, even seeing. Jesus allows the disciple to touch the wounds of his healing, and Thomas's faith is strengthened. And the Lord responds, "Because you have seen me, you have believed. Blessed are those who have not seen and yet believe" (20:29).

He is speaking of you and me.

We believe based on the testimony of these eyewitnesses. We believe based on the testimony to our own spirits of the Spirit who has breathed out the holy Scriptures. We believe even though we cannot see. We believe that someday we will see.

Christ took all of that tangibility to heaven, where he maintains it today. It is one reason, I'm convinced, he's given us the ordinance of the Lord's Supper, telling us the bread and wine are his body and his blood. I'm not a transubstantiationist, believing that the bread and wine of the meal are transformed *literally* into Christ's flesh and blood, but the tangibility of the elements of the communion meal are nevertheless a means of grace reminding us of the grace of Christ's cross. The fact we can see them, hold them, and taste them is a reminder that Jesus is tangibly real.

One day soon, he will return. All will see him then (Rev. 1:7). Our friendship with Jesus now is driven by the surety of this hope we share with Job:

> But I know that my Redeemer lives,
> and at the end he will stand on the dust.
> Even after my skin has been destroyed,
> yet I will see God in my flesh.
> I will see him myself;
> my eyes will look at him, and not as a stranger.
>   (Job 19:25–27)

No, not as a stranger. As a friend.

In contemplating the overwhelming sweetness of his present faith filled with his future hope, Job goes on to cry, "My heart longs within me" (v. 27). That's the cry of one who knows God. It's the cry of those who experience closeness with Jesus. Job is undoubtedly a servant of God (1:8), but this longing of the heart is a sign of a friendship spirituality.

The Divine Dialogue

A preacher friend of mine once said that every pastor ought to know what the carpet in their office smells like. It's a strange statement, to be sure, but he was trying to encourage the posture of the pastor as one of prayer. When I was pastoring, I took the application literally and began regularly praying facedown in my church office. I could tell you what the carpet smelled like.

There was something about that unique posture that also helped my prayers. The out-of-the-ordinary demeanor of lying prostrate on the ground heightened my sense of the reality of talking to God.

These days I have to remind myself regularly that when I pray I'm not just throwing words into outer space. No, I'm engaging in my part of a very real conversation with a very real friend. Just because I can't see him doesn't mean he's not real. And it doesn't mean that I don't want to see him!

The heart of friendship spirituality is one that longs to see Jesus. This heart is frequently overflowing with desire to be with Jesus. It doesn't need to be in the Sandia Mountains or facedown on the carpet in a church office to experience this longing. To be friends with Jesus means picking up anywhere and everywhere. It means taking advantage of the ready access we have by grace through faith to the very place where God is (Eph. 2:18). "Therefore," the author of Hebrews tells us, "let us approach the throne of grace with boldness, so that we may receive mercy and find grace to help us in time of need" (4:16).

We can, in the spiritual sense, at any time have a conversation with God. We can pursue active friendship with Jesus. This friendship is enjoyed primarily through what I call "the divine dialogue." This is the normative means by which we hear from God and God hears from us. This is how it works: we hear from God in his Word.

If you have access to a reliable copy of the Bible, you may never say that God is silent with you. He has spoken authoritatively, thoroughly, and effectively to us in the Scriptures. But we must approach the Scriptures with this in mind. We can come to the Bible for more knowledge, and that's fine. Its facts are impeccable. We can come to the Bible for artistry, and that's fine. Its words are beautiful. We can come to the Bible for instructions on the religious life, and that too is fine. The law of God is holy and glorious. But if we don't come to the Word of God *for life*, we run the risk of dying smart, entertained, and religious.

There's a marked difference between seeing the Bible as a resource and seeing the Bible as sustenance (Matt. 4:4).

Reading the Bible is how we listen to Jesus as one would listen to a friend. Because the whole Bible is about Jesus. Yes, the whole Bible. Not just the New Testament. Not just the Gospels. Not just the red letters. The whole thing. "You pore over the Scriptures," Jesus himself says to the religious folks, "because you think you have eternal life in them, and yet they testify about me" (John 5:39). The Scriptures he's referring to are what we now call the Old Testament.

Further, after his resurrection, Jesus sidles up next to some of his disciples on the road to Emmaus and "beginning with Moses and all the Prophets, he interpreted for them the things concerning himself in all the Scriptures" (Luke 24:27). As Paul says in 2 Corinthians 1:20, "Every one of God's promises is 'Yes' in [Jesus]."

Do you approach your Scripture reading this way? Do you approach your pursuit of theological knowledge this way? Do you approach your contemplation of God's holy commands this way? It's the difference between a servant spirituality and a friendship spirituality.

Every time we open the Bible, then, it's a kind of burning bush moment. We're on holy ground and standing in the very presence of God, hearing his very voice. If you want Jesus to speak to you, listen to him in the Word. He is not short of words!

Secondarily, we speak to God through prayer. There are a million ways to go about this sacred practice, but Jesus gives us some basic instructions in what we traditionally call the Lord's Prayer. The thoroughgoing sense of this template prayer is humble submission and childlike access. In prayer, we exalt God and commit ourselves to his will. In prayer, we ask for things—big things like the promised coming of the kingdom and heaven "made real" on earth and little things like daily needs. (Of course, for some people at all times and for all people at some times, those daily needs may not feel like little things at all.) There's a reverent formality to the Lord's Prayer, which is instructive for us. But there's also an openhearted intimacy in it. When we're instructed to pray for forgiveness, and we bring the relational conflicts we may have with others before God's throne, we're getting to the most vulnerable and desperate part of ourselves. If we're being honest.

Elsewhere, I have called this part of the divine dialogue "spilling your guts." This is what I wrote previously in my book *The Imperfect Disciple*:

Before the holy God of the universe we can finally and totally be our real selves.

Look, prayer is spilling your guts. It doesn't have to be pretty. It doesn't have to be tidy. It doesn't have to be particularly eloquent or even particularly intelligent. But the Bible is how God speaks to us and prayer is how we speak to God. These two rhythms form the dynamic of our friendship with the God of the universe. You can't be good friends with someone you don't listen to, and you can't be good friends with someone you don't talk to. So we go about our personal devotions by studying the Bible to hear what God would say to us and then praying to God that he would forgive us for our hard-heartedness against his Word and empower us to understand it better and make it resonate more deeply in our hearts. Spilling our guts in prayer is how we process God's words to us. Prayer is how we interact with our friend Jesus.[2]

What I'm trying to stress is that while prayer must be reverent and submissive, it must also be personal and real. The Lord hears all of our cruddy prayers. The Spirit even prays for us when we don't quite have the words (Rom. 8:26). So we don't have to be afraid to speak to our friend Jesus. We can open up to him. We can confess freely. We don't have to pretend. We can't impress him, and we certainly can't fool him.

In 1 John 1:7, the apostle says that if we walk in the light, we'll have fellowship with our brothers and sisters. I think he means that if we're honest about our sins and our struggles and our very selves, we can be sure we have real relationships with the people around us. Too many of us put our religious self on when it's time to go to church, and the result is that our church doesn't know the real us. They just know the religious avatar we send to church in our place. In the same way, if we want to know the real Jesus, we should trust that we can bring our real selves before him.

So don't let the label "divine dialogue" throw you off. I'm referring simply to the reliable practice we could just call "talking to Jesus." Don't let his invisibility in these moments become an intellectual obstacle to spiritually sensing his presence. You can pull up a chair or sit under a tree or lie in your bed or drive to work or sit on the bus or train or at the table in the cafeteria or in your kitchen and talk to Jesus. We listen to him speaking through his Word. We speak to him through our prayers. And it's a real conversation with a real person. It's a real conversation with a real person who loves us, desires closeness with us, and wants us to know him. He knows we cannot be changed into his goodness apart from being friends with him.

So let's hide nothing in our hearts from him. (It's not possible anyway.) Let's relate to Jesus as a real person—trusting that he's real and entrusting our real self to his grace. Let our prayers be pure, 100 percent, unadulterated stupid us. For our friend Jesus has promised us: "Blessed are the pure in heart, for they will see God" (Matt. 5:8).

3

Nearer than
Our Next Breath

(Jesus the Close Friend)

The sea-sick passenger shall come to land; Christ will be the
first that will meet you on the shore.

Samuel Rutherford, *The Loveliness of Christ*[1]

There is no friend closer than Jesus. As we follow him, he
never strides too far ahead. He never dodges or ditches
us. If we are weary, he slows. If we pull up lame, he stops. If
we wander, he circles back. He won't let us be lost.

Hopefully it's been well established to the believing heart
that Jesus is a real person. But to say that he's real says nothing of his closeness. My Aunt Coylene is real. But if I wanted
to have a cup of coffee with her, one of us would have to

travel 1,100 miles to do it. Jesus isn't an idea or ideology, we agree; he is a real person. But he lives up in heaven. Even if we could travel there, it must be more than a million miles away. To our earthbound minds, heaven seems impossible to reach.

But this isn't exactly the concept of heaven the Scriptures hold out to us. Yes, we have the language itself to contend with—it is named, after all, for *the heavens*, for the skies. When the ancients speak of "going to heaven," they always refer to an ascent. In 1 Kings 18, when Elijah defeats the prophets of Baal, the fire from heaven comes *down*. In 2 Kings 2, when Elijah is taken to heaven, the whirlwind takes him *up*. And Jesus *ascended* to heaven. But this spatial language belies the hyperspatial dimensionality of the place.

Heaven, properly understood, is the place of God's manifest presence. It's the place, if it's even right to call it a *place*, where God's will is perfectly done. And if God is omnipresent, heaven must, in some sense, be all around us, or at least in some spiritual way parallel or alongside or embedded within or surrounding our spatial-temporal world. Heaven, then, isn't some ethereal palace in the clouds or far away in outer space. It's instead nearer than we expect. It's the place of God's presence. And while it's perfectly fine to speak as though heaven is a place to which we're going, we should also think of heaven as a place that's coming to us.

When the Holy Spirit conceives the Christ-child in Mary's virgin womb, we can rightly say that heaven has come down. When Jesus begins his earthly ministry, the announcement is that the kingdom of God (or "kingdom of heaven," to use Matthew's vernacular) is "at hand." Heaven has in fact come near (Matt. 3:2; Luke 10:9). And the blessed hope held out for us in the New Testament isn't exactly our going to heaven when we die but rather Christ returning to us, ushering in a new heaven and new earth that he gloriously brings with him. The coming closeness of God is a constant, reverberating theme in the Scriptures.

Several years ago, I found myself adrift in a bewildering and burdensome season of loneliness. This happened during a time of intense ministry, in which I was increasingly overwhelmed by expectations I couldn't meet, disappointments I couldn't shake, and obligations I couldn't avoid. It was a serious period of grief and mourning too. The dark night of the soul was an everyday occurrence. I had close friends, but none close by. The friends I thought I had nearby grew distant. It seemed that all the people who once had my back had exited the room while it was turned. And the hard and bitter things I had to face, I had to face alone.

Many pastors will tell you one of the most difficult things in ministry isn't the difficult things but having to navigate them alone. I don't exactly know why this is the case—and believe me, I've thought a lot about it—but it's frequently very difficult for ministers to make or keep friends. In this particular season of loneliness, I didn't even feel like I could talk to my wife about my struggles, as she was facing many struggles of her own and I didn't want to burden her any further. I decided to suck it up and let whatever was happening to me just play itself out.

Loneliness has a compounding effect. The more alone you feel, the more hopeless you become. I'm an introvert by nature, a constant internal processor. Normally being alone isn't a big problem for me. But being alone and feeling alone aren't always the same thing. I felt completely and utterly alone.

However, this wasn't the first time I'd experienced something like this. That period of depression I told you about in the introduction was a profound season of loneliness. In some respects, it wasn't just the awful circumstances of those days but my having to sort through those circumstances alone that was the worst thing that ever happened to me. But my encounter with the living God in that guest bedroom was transformative and empowering for me ever after. I had encountered the enduring friendship of my Savior. Now, I was a believer at that time—indeed, my only hope in those days was a feeble clinging to the hem of Christ's garment—but I was suddenly overcome by a new awakening to the gospel.

And so, because of that earlier experience, while I was going through this more recent challenge of loneliness, I was more prepared to acknowledge that my feelings were an illusion. I knew the Lord was at hand, even if I struggled to sense him. These memories didn't make my feelings of loneliness immediately go away, but I was closer to hope than I had been before, if only because I knew from experience that the deep and dense valley I'd fallen into was no hindrance to my Savior.

King David exulted in the ever-presence of God this way:

> Where can I go to escape your Spirit?
> Where can I flee from your presence?
> If I go up to heaven, you are there;
> if I make my bed in Sheol, you are there.
> If I fly on the wings of the dawn
> and settle down on the western horizon,
> even there your hand will lead me;
> your right hand will hold on to me.

If I say, "Surely the darkness will hide me,
and the light around me will be night"—
even the darkness is not dark to you.
The night shines like the day;
darkness and light are alike to you. (Ps. 139:7–12)

In times of burdensome solitude, it's always helpful to contemplate the transcendence of God, but perhaps doubly so his immanence.

Loneliness, oppression, and perhaps even depression were all feelings David couldn't easily shake. But he also trusted that he couldn't shake God. It's in this way that we, like him, can begin to see how Christ's deity and all its attributes makes for better news than we expected.

The Gospel of Omnipresence

In 2021, the government of Japan hired its very first Minister of Loneliness. His name is Tetsushi Sakamoto, and the prime minister has tasked him with leading the government's plans to combat an epidemic of isolation in their country that has led to a staggering increase in the suicide rate. Journalist Katie Warren writes:

Loneliness has long been an issue in Japan, often discussed alongside "hikikomori," or people who live in extreme social isolation. People have worked to create far-ranging solutions to this issue: Engineers in Japan previously designed a robot to hold someone's hand when they're lonely and one man charges people to "do nothing" except keep them company.[2]

These are some creative ways, certainly, to combat a unique new health crisis that in our post-COVID world has now become global. Even before the pandemic, however, the warning signs for this growing risk were multiplying. The *Boston Globe* reported in 2017 on findings that loneliness posed a greater health risk to middle-aged men than smoking or obesity.[3]

I was speaking recently with a pastor friend of mine, Justin Buzzard, who ministers in the Silicon Valley of California, and he told me that the two biggest touchpoints for beginning gospel conversations with the large and diverse mass of unbelievers in his mission field are anxiety and loneliness. For the most part, his missional context is made up of young, ambitious, intelligent, and successful people. They work for Google and Tesla and Facebook and Zoom. They live in a beautiful part of the state and either make lots of money or are on their way to doing so. And they feel incredibly alone. The shutdowns from the COVID pandemic only exacerbated people's sense of isolation and alienation, too, and Justin mentioned something I hadn't thought of before: even the garden-variety "background socialization" of just going to the grocery store or standing in line at the bank or coffee shop or sitting across from people at restaurants was all effectively shut down in California. Those who were eager to work from home to avoid long commutes eventually began to express missing the social matrixes of their workplaces and their weekend recreation, once government shutdowns forbade those options. We've seen this perhaps most profoundly when children who were used to the steady socialization of school were suddenly sent home for months on end.

We were made for relationship. We were made to connect. Even introverts like me aren't truly wired to do life alone. I'm sorry, Simon and Garfunkel, but I'm not a rock, and I'm not an island.

Soon after his making, Adam is told by his Creator that it's not good for him to be alone. Eve is then made as "a helper corresponding to him" (Gen. 2:18). This scene obviously establishes the goodness of the gift of marriage, but it speaks to a larger reality too. We were wired for togetherness even before sin entered the world. Even before the fall, Adam couldn't say he was self-sufficient.

But even our God, who *is* self-sufficient (the theological term for this idea is *aseity*, which refers to the fact that God isn't dependent on any person or thing beside his own self in order to exist), exists as a Trinity. Now, this doesn't mean that each Person of the Trinity is lacking something that the other Persons supply or that each Person is somehow a dependent "part" making up the whole of the Trinity. Christians believe that each Person of the Trinity—Father, Son, and Holy Spirit—is fully and eternally God, that they all simultaneously and equally share the same essence. But it *does* mean that our eternal God exists in relationship in his very self.

For man and woman to be made in God's image (1:27), then, is in part to be made for relationship—with other men and women, and with God himself. The relationships with other men and women part, this side of the fall of humankind, can be exceedingly difficult. We see it in the way we struggle with friendship, the way so many friendships don't seem to last. We certainly see it in the way marriages so often fall apart. Even the marriages that do last prevail only after making forgiveness and grace high priorities. Relationships are difficult primarily because we're sinners! And having sin in us means that as natural as our need to extend outward is, our selfish bend inward is just as natural.

But relationships with other men and women are difficult also because we're increasingly divided by space and time in the twenty-first century. God, however, isn't bound by these. Any person who desires a relationship with God can have one, precisely because he isn't out in some ethereal space across some untraversable distance.

If you and I want a relationship with God, we can have one, no matter where we are, because God is omnipresent. He's literally everywhere. When Paul sees their statue to an unknown god, he tells the Greeks in the Areopagus that the real God isn't far from any one of us (Acts 17:27).

Jesus Christ is fully human, yes. But he's also fully God. This necessarily means that Jesus Christ is both incarnate and omnipresent. If he weren't truly incarnate, he wouldn't be truly human. But if he were not also omnipresent, he wouldn't be truly God. Because God cannot *not* be omnipresent. Omnipresence is one of God's attributes. Thus, the God-Man is both in the flesh and simultaneously *everywhere*.

Historically this concept has been referred to as the *extra calvinisticum*, which I always joke means "a little bit of extra Calvin." But the Latin term simply refers to the fact that the incarnation wasn't a limiting of the Son but, in a way, an act of addition (as in, "adding something extra"), and it's named after John Calvin as he was perhaps the idea's most influential advocate. Literally, the phrase means "Calvin's theology of the beyond." (Calvin didn't invent or innovate the concept, of course; he just happens to be credited with developing it in a thorough and impactful way.)

While some believers may struggle with this idea when first contemplating it, even those who agree with it may further struggle to comprehend its benefit. What difference does the *extra calvinisticum* make in our everyday life? Isn't it just one of those bits of theological trivia like "How many angels can dance on the head of a pin?" or "Did Adam and Eve have belly buttons?"

No. Affirming Christ's simultaneous incarnation and omnipresence has huge implications not just for our intellectual grasp of a right theology of God but for our spiritual grasp of a right relationship with him! Jesus isn't simply out there somewhere. He's not in the heavenly distance, detached from our experiences and concerns, any more than God the Father is some glorified Santa Claus looking down on us from afar with occasional bemusement. That kind of thinking is more along the lines of the boring, ineffectual theology of deism.

What Christians believe is that the risen and glorified Jesus Christ ascended to heaven, where he sits at the right hand of the Father, *and* is also really present among us. Indeed, if you're a Christian, he is present *within* you.

When Jesus tells his disciples before his ascension "I am with you always," he doesn't simply mean that he'll be with them metaphorically, in their memories. He means that he will always be *with them*.

Christian, he will always be *with you*. Indeed, he's promised that he will "never leave you nor forsake you" (Heb. 13:5 ESV).

Do you see how this biblical way of thinking can have a huge impact on your experience of friendship with Jesus?

At the very least, it means that when you're praying to the Father through Christ, Christ is truly there with you, listening as closely as a trusted friend or beloved brother. It means that when we're reading our Bibles and listening to his voice, Christ is right next to us, looking at the text alongside us, speaking those words to our hearts. And it means that in those painfully common times when we don't particularly *feel* near to Jesus, he isn't actually far away from us.

That's the beautiful paradox of Christ's commitment of grace to us and the good news of omnipresence for us: our distance from him doesn't necessitate his distance from us. Even while we may drift day after day, further and further away, we still discover he's always been closer than our next breath.

The doctrine of God's omnipresence, registered through the lens of Christ's gospel, means that Jesus will always be near to us in grace. It means that his righteousness given to us isn't merely past tense but eternally present. The gospel of omnipresence is that the personal goodness and mercy of Christ himself will be following you all the days of your life (Ps. 23:6). You wake up to his approving presence; you go to bed at night to his approving presence.

If you've repented of your sin and placed your faith in Jesus, his omnipresence is good news. It's a reminder that he always lives to come close by in love. Look, the whole point of the incarnation was God's manifest presence drawing near to us. He has come to dwell among us.

He won't even keep a superior detachment from sinners! He gets up close and personal. He touches people's sores. He holds their hands. He puts his spit in people's eyes. You couldn't keep him at arm's length if you tried. You certainly cannot cordon him off from your life with chains of flesh or velvet ropes of religion.

Throughout the Gospels and even today, Jesus is constantly stepping on toes, touching nerves, and getting under skin. Is it any wonder, then, that his felt presence isn't experienced in temples or tabernacles or shrines built by human hands but in the very hearts of his people (Eph. 3:17), that the kingdom of heaven isn't just out there or even near us, but *in* our midst (Luke 17:21)?

Christ is in fact nearer than your next breath.

Here, There, and Everywhere

The gospel gem of union with Christ is perhaps the major facet of the gospel uniting the whole of the New Testament. It's implicitly proclaimed every time we see phrases such as "in him" or "in Christ" or "with him"—to be found in Christ, to be raised with Christ, to move and live and have our being in Christ, to be crucified with Christ and seated with him in the heavenly places, to be hidden with Christ in God.

In John 15, Jesus tells his disciples that they're the branches and he's the vine, and that they must "remain in him" or "abide in him." This is all doctrine of union talk. In John 17, a picture is cast that Christ doesn't just advocate for us as a defense attorney—though he does that too (see chapter 6)—but grafts us into himself. But further: by faith, the sinner saved by grace is spiritually inextricable from Jesus. His Spirit indwells us. And we are said to dwell in him.

How is this? How is it that he would be, spiritually speaking, inside of us? And how is it that we would also be, spiritually speaking, inside of him?

71

Well, think of the temple in the ancient days. The Holy of Holies was the place where God's presence specially dwelled. But it wouldn't be accurate to say God's wholeness was solely located in that physical space. God is omnipresent. He can't *not* be omnipresent. So God was outside the temple and everywhere. But also he dwelled specially in the temple. This is a corollary to the indwelling presence of Christ in believers. We are in him. But he is also specially in us.

Think of a matryoshka doll. You know, one of those Russian nesting dolls, where you open it up and there's an increasingly smaller doll inside? Well, picture just three dolls. The middle doll is us. We are inside the larger doll of Christ, so that when you open him up, you find us. But when you open us up, you find the third doll resting inside of us is him again.

Our inextricability from Christ through union with him by faith is one way we know that we belong to God. This is how we know the Father is *keeping us*. He is guarding us, and not one of us will be lost.

Speaking of Russia, as I write this Ukraine is defending their nation from a bloody invasion. A few months ago, as Russian invaders stepped onto Ukrainian soil, I happened to see a photo online of a group of Ukrainian Christians in a circle in Kharkiv Square, joined in prayer. I was struck by two things in contemplating that photo. The first thing was the sheer vulnerability of these men and women. Seven or eight human beings armed with nothing but winter coats are definitely no match for small arms fire, much less heavy artillery. But the second thing was the sheer *power* of these people. For Christians, to be found in Christ, to be guarded and kept by him, is—in all the ways that ultimately and eternally matter—to be utterly unconquerable. Those Ukrainian Christians out in the open praying could've easily been blown to pieces. But they also represented a collection of the strongest power on earth: souls kept by Christ.

Oh, sure, we can be killed. But we cannot be conquered.

As Paul says in Colossians 3:3, our "life is hidden with Christ in God." And if we're hidden with Christ in God, we're as secure as Christ is.

Now, how secure do you think Christ is? He's an unconquerable foundation, an eternal foundation.

Puritan Samuel Rutherford wrote that when we finally make it to the safety of shore, Christ will be the first one to greet us.[4] But the truth is, Christ has been on our storm-tossed ship all along. Even if we're thrown from its bow into the foamy darkness, he'll be with us. There's no place we can go that our friend Jesus won't be first beside us.

Oh, but you may naturally wonder, *Why in the world would he do all this* for me? This is what the soul will say when it has been supernaturally humbled by the reality of its sin in light of God's holiness. So good job. But remember the good news that God loves sinners. Jesus died for sinners! He isn't looking for awesome people to unite to himself. He isn't looking for put-together people for his Spirit to indwell. He isn't looking for religious people to become brand ambassadors for him.

Jesus came to save sinners. He came to unite to himself people who could add nothing to him. He sends his Spirit to indwell people who are intimately familiar with emptiness. He's looking for the last, least, and lost to bear the brandmarks of himself (Gal. 6:17) as his beloved brothers and sisters.

"But I just keep screwing up," you might say. "I'm a mess."

Still the good news endures. Because of the gracious reality of the sinner's spiritual union with Jesus, what's true of us apart from him cannot ultimately define us in God's sight. Because we are in Christ, the Father sees us through the perfection of his Son. What ultimately defines us now is Jesus's goodness, because what's true of him is now considered true of us too. As it pertains to righteousness, our lives are so indistinguishable from Christ's that Paul is prompted to say, "If we are faithless, he remains faithful, for he cannot deny himself" (2 Tim. 2:13).

The omnipresence of God becomes a fortress for those who enjoy union with Christ. And the doctrines of omnipresence and union can together become hallowed ground for affectionate worship, because they remind us that we may relate to our friend Jesus here, there, and everywhere. There is literally no place we'll be without our sweetest friend, because he has lovingly lashed himself to us, whatever may come. And whatever comes, because of him, cannot overcome us.

Isn't this the kind of friend you'd want to know intimately? If he's always close by and always cares for you, wouldn't you be crazy not to make friends with him?

King David writes, "I always let the LORD guide me. Because he is at my right hand, I will not be shaken" (Ps. 16:8). The first sentence in that verse can be translated more literally as, "I place the LORD in front of me always."

He's always there. He's always inviting us to hold him as first in our hearts. Jesus is worth cherishing as the truest treasure. He's worth trusting as the kindest counselor. He's worth worshiping as the glorious Lord. And he's worth knowing as the dearest friend.

He is sweetly calling everyone who would follow him to relationally "place him" in front of themselves always.

The Felt Presence of Christ

When Jesus walked the earth in the flesh, how close did he get to those who needed him?

He came close enough to heal their illnesses and bear their diseases (Ps. 103:3; Matt. 4:23). He touched the wounds of lepers. He grasped the limbs of the lame. He pressed flesh (Mark 5:24). He held hands (v. 41; 9:27). He took children into his lap. He let his disciples lean against his chest. If he'd had wings, he would've put the whole city under them (Matt. 23:37).

Jesus came close enough to bear our sin. Close enough that when he died, we died with him. When he was raised, we were raised with him. We are at this very moment seated with him in the heavenly places (Eph. 2:6). We are—*present tense*—hidden with him in God (Col. 3:3). If he is closer to us than our very skin, we have every right now, by his grace, to pursue deep communion with God through him at any time.

Too many professing Christians suffer from shallow, stale religiosity or a heartless, unaffectionate theologizing, because they haven't made it a priority to know the felt presence of Christ. Now, I'm not referring merely to spiritual feelings, though those are important in their own way. By "felt presence of Christ," I'm referring to the practice—driven by the divine dialogue—of communion with the one with whom we have union. In fact, we can experience communion with Christ because of our union with him. This is accomplished and authorized by *his* work, not ours. We don't summon him or stir him up or somehow activate him. Rather, by grace through faith, we submit our wills to his, taking his yoke and burden upon ourselves, and embrace the reality that he is a real person.

"Felt presence" refers to experiential knowledge of the God who is real through his Spirit who is real in the Son who is real. We may not see him face-to-face as Moses did, but we still speak to him face-to-face. For he is always with us, always near, always looking at us with the readiness of love and the warmth of one who would give—*has given*—everything necessary to be close to us.

In Luke 24, after the Lord comes near to the disciples on the road to Emmaus and tells them everything about himself in the Scriptures, these men aren't simply engaged intellectually. They don't hear Jesus out and respond, "Ah, that's rather interesting. I'd never looked at it that way before, Jesus." No, they're stirred to worship! Their very hearts burn within their chests (v. 32).

This kind of holy heartburn isn't necessary to experience closeness with Jesus, of course, but it's certainly a worthy desire. We go to church services expecting to feel something in the singing and preaching. We watch movies or sports and expect to become emotionally invested. We listen to music and become moved to dance or cry or drive over the speed limit. Should we not engage the divine dialogue and expect to be moved to, as 1 Peter 1:8 says, "rejoice with inexpressible and glorious joy"?

There's nothing wrong and everything right with wanting to feel our friendship with Jesus.

And yet the felt presence of Christ is a more profound experience than some kind of "godly goose bumps." We don't have to feel particularly moved by the music at our church service to authentically exalt God through our participation in it. And we don't have to feel a particular way to engage in friendship with Jesus. In fact, the conversational experience of the divine dialogue *is itself* the felt presence of Christ. He's truly present in the meditating on his Word. And he's truly present in the intercession of our prayers.

Jesus is our Immanuel—God *with* us. And Jesus is the God who is *for* us. And he's the God who lives *in* us. One of the most wonderful implications of these accumulated prepositions is that, despite our sin and stupidity, God is committed to seeing us through to the end. His Spirit will bear fruit in our hearts. His Son will be reflected in our lives. The faith he pioneered in us, he will perfect (Heb. 12:2). This too is the felt presence of Christ.

When you hear the Word preached faithfully, that's the felt presence of Christ. When you're encouraged and edified by the spiritual songs of your congregation, that's the felt presence of Christ. When you share the table of fellowship with brothers and sisters, that's the felt presence of Christ. When you generously give or sacrificially serve, when you do for others what you'd wish done for yourself, that's the felt presence of Christ. Certainly, at the church's communion, when you eat that bread and drink that cup, that's the felt presence of Christ.

And when you get alone in that messy room and pray your messy prayers and try to make head or tail of a confusing passage in Ezekiel—yes, even that is the felt presence of Christ.

Our feelings are no barrier to him. Even our sins are no obstacle for him!

Luke 15 opens with this testimony: "All the tax collectors and sinners were approaching to listen to him. And the Pharisees and scribes were complaining, 'This man welcomes sinners and eats with them'" (vv. 1–2). Thank God! He makes close friends even out of sinners.

There is hope for you and me, then. We're not much to look at—spiritually speaking, at least. But our lovely Savior will share his loveliness with us.

It's hard for us to stay on the right track. But our trusty Shepherd will see us safe through the darkest valleys and narrowest roads. We don't reach out as often or as eagerly as we should. But our faithful friend remains ever patient, ever gracious, ever ready to receive us. We are great sinners, but he is a greater Savior.

If you want the felt presence of Christ, pursue mindfulness of that sin and conviction over it. Ask the Lord to reveal any dark corner of your heart he wills. Don't sweep any of it under the rug. Turn to face it. Trace the dark line of nasty thoughts and perverted lusts and every assorted un-glory within you that stands in opposition to the holy God all the way to the point of their deserved ends. You will find that this line, crooked as its path may be, inevitably comes to a place that looks like a skull. It's a place of death, the dreadful place of the proper accounting for the wages of sin. And there atop that skull, at the pinnacle of the accumulated pile of your insurmountable debts, see your friend Jesus. See him utterly poured out to make it all right.

He has felt what we ought to feel, and in doing so pardons what we don't. He has gone where we wouldn't dare to bring us where we'd only dreamed. And he'll never, ever kick us out (John 6:37).

No, not even you.

"Draw near to God," therefore, "and he will draw near to you" (James 4:8).

On the Unsucking of Your Gut

(Jesus the Comforting Friend)

He wants you as you are; He does not want anything from you, a sacrifice, a work; He wants you alone.

Dietrich Bonhoeffer, *Life Together*[1]

There is no friend so comforting as Jesus. There's no friend so able to accept us as we are, so free with his enjoyment of our company, who is so much at ease with himself that he's satisfied in our presence despite our inabilities and incapacities. There's no friend more comforting than one you don't feel like you constantly have to impress.

I've come to evaluate the state of my friendships through this lens: How easy is it with this person to not have to *be* anything? If I'm hanging with someone from church, am I able to naturally relax with them or do I always have to have my "pastor hat" on? (Wearing the pastor hat isn't a bad thing; it just isn't conducive to natural friendship.) If I'm visiting with someone in my line of work, whether a peer or a superior, I'm usually thinking about how to gain their approval. With most acquaintances I meet along the way of life, I have two primary modes of relating: impress or ignore.

That may sound shallow (and it is), but if you're honest, I bet most of your interactions with acquaintances fall into one of those two categories as well.

Finding the friend you don't want to ignore but don't have to impress can seem daunting. This is part of the reason I think real friendship more often seems to "just happen" than is the result of some concerted effort to "make friends." I've found that it's easier to be a friend *to* somebody than it is to be friends *with* anybody. Have you ever had someone tell you, whether by word or action, that you're going to be best friends? It doesn't work, does it? Just because you can be a friend *to* anybody doesn't mean you can be friends *with* anybody.

The reason it's hard to be friends with somebody who's insisting on the friendship is that the whole relationship is predicated on expectation. It's a form of relational legalism. They have a need to be your friend, and they're insisting you share that need. But this isn't how real friendships begin, even between people who need friends!

A couple of years back I posted an informal poll from my Twitter feed, asking how many men age forty and over were still good friends with friends they had in high school. Over a thousand guys replied, and 45 percent said they didn't have any friendships left from high school. Only 25 percent indicated they were still close with any friends from high school. (The remaining 30 percent of respondents said they were now only acquaintances or only connected on social media with friends from high school.) The results made me feel very blessed, because thirty years after high school, I'm still close friends with three of the guys I was close to back then.

I met Eric (who goes by Bird) in gym class. I connected with his uncle Mark (who goes by Blo and is only a few years older than us) through hanging out with Bird. We'd play basketball or football every weekend together. I met my friend Bill at church. Bill is probably ten years older than me, but we hit it off on a youth group trip to Colorado one summer when I was a student ministry intern and he was a volunteer, and we've been tight ever since. I introduced Bill to Bird and Blo, and later, after I moved to another state, we started a group blog called *The Thinklings*, into which I roped a few other friends, including my buddy Phil.

Three decades from the start of this friendship circle, we talk almost daily via ongoing text thread and get together in person at least once a year to stay up all night, grill steaks, and talk about everything. It's one of the deepest blessings of my life.

When we were young, we'd talk about music and sports and books. We'd debate theology (Calvinism vs. Arminianism and eschatology are two perennial favorite subjects) and talk way too much about cryptozoology (we're pretty divided on the evidence for Bigfoot). We still talk about all these things today! But as we're all middle-aged now, most of our serious conversations revolve around concerns about our kids, the health (or sadly, the deaths) of parents and other friends, and the state of our marriages and churches and jobs.

I knew every one of these guys before I'd ever published a book. I knew these guys before I was ever invited to speak at a conference. I knew these guys before I planted a church. And I knew these guys before I made a mess of my marriage and went through depression and countless ministry and relational crises.

We all knew each other before any of us made anything of ourselves, which is why these are the easiest friendships in the world. They aren't impressed by me, and I honestly don't care. To them, I'm just Jared (although among the Thinklings I go by Rod). I have no desire with these friends to be anything or prove anything or, a lot of the time, even *do* anything. I just love sitting around for hours with them and talking. Some of my more recent friends may find this astonishing, because I've developed a pretty good reputation for limiting my human interaction!

To this perception, I plead guilty. Sort of. I do enjoy being with (most) people, but as an introvert, I can find it taxing. Again, even if I enjoy the time spent, it can still feel draining. I need to recharge through rest and solitude. (This is in contrast to extroversion, which seems to function the other way: relational interactions are themselves felt as replenishment.) But with close friends like the Thinklings, plus a few others I've known for a long while, my capacity for fellowship seems almost bottomless.

I've thought a lot about how this can be the case. How is it that a frequently antisocial introvert like me wouldn't be able to get enough time with certain people? And I think it's because the time spent with these people is tantamount to time spent alone—meaning I can just be myself. I can breathe, I can slouch, I can unsuck my gut.

Jesus is a friend like this. What's beautiful about friendship with Jesus is that it's predicated on his own relational foreknowledge of us (Rom. 8:29). He's not only known you since you were young, he's known you since before there *was* a you!

He's known you before you even felt the need to talk big about yourself. For me, this started pretty early. I remember two lies I told when I very young. When I was five or six, I remember telling a babysitter I'd been to Disney World, when in fact I hadn't. She insisted that I was making it up. I didn't budge. I told her all about the rides I'd been on and characters I'd seen. Even when caught in the lie, I refused to give it up. My need to entertain was greater than my desire to be known. Of course, I was just a kid. As an adult, I have less of an excuse.

When I was in the third grade, I remember telling my dad over a succession of family dinners that I had come in first place every day when we had to run laps during PE. I wasn't a slow kid, but I wasn't close to the fastest. Yet I told him I was. These exercises weren't even races, but I told him I won them. Every single day. Why did I do that? The answer's pretty easy. I was eight years old and wanted my dad to think I was good at something.

Jesus knew me before I started thinking of myself as a big deal. Even more importantly, he knows that I struggle with needing to feel like a big deal. And he's friends with me anyway. He knows that I have a deep wound of disapproval in my heart, that I secretly want to be noticed but then feel very guilty when I am, that I'm a huge mess of contradictions and dysfunctions, of needs and neuroses. He knows that I'm a black hole of sin. And he's friends with me anyway.

There is no friend so comforting as Jesus.

Hide and Seek

My friend Ray once told me we have the choice of being impressive or being known, but we can't be both. I'm not sure I agree (especially since I'm impressed by people who aren't trying to impress!), but I get his basic point. What we try to do with our efforts to impress is subterfuge. We put up a façade to hide our real selves from others.

This is what's so weird about the performative nature of so much social media. We know more about each other than we ever cared (or ought) to, but we still don't know each other. We know only the carefully curated versions of ourselves we present. Ironically, all our attempts at being "seen" are actually attempts to hide.

I do know a little bit about hiding while desperately wanting to belong.

I've never shared this publicly before, but it appears I was born with a congenital condition known as *pectus excavatum.* This basically means that my sternum, which in a normal skeleton extends through the rib cage perpendicular to or slightly angled outward from the body, angles inward toward my heart. The effect on most with the condition is the appearance of a sunken chest. In my case, it's like a softball sized "bowl" in the middle of my chest.

This wasn't very noticeable when I was a small child, but I began to notice my chest was built differently from the other boys probably in late elementary school, early junior high. I was a very thin kid growing up, so I think my family and I just assumed it was a feature of my being skinny. But I remember asking my mom to ask the doctor about it during an appointment when I was probably thirteen or fourteen.

The doctor took a look at my chest and diagnosed me as, you guessed it, skinny. He said the impression in my chest would diminish as I got older and gained more muscle and fat. Well, I got older and gained more muscle. Then, later in my adulthood, more fat. The bowl in my chest did not diminish but only became more pronounced.

A few years ago I finally went to Google to figure out my particular freakishness. That's when I discovered the medical term for it. I felt somewhat encouraged, actually, as a lot of people with *pectus excavatum* suffer from heart and lung issues that haven't affected me. The encroaching sternum can threaten healthy functioning of the organs the rib cage is meant to protect. I don't have any of those issues. But I do have the stigma of growing up with a sunken chest and being incredibly embarrassed about it. (Also, I learned that one of my favorite actors, Joel Kinnaman, suffered from the same condition but underwent an elaborate surgery to correct it.)

As an adolescent, I stopped taking my shirt off at the pool or beach. I'm sure folks wondered why a skinny kid would wear a shirt to swim, but I hoped they'd think it was to avoid sunburn. I loved playing basketball and football, and I was a pretty good athlete, usually good enough to be first or second pick when teams were chosen. But when the boys would play "shirts and skins," I had to bow out for fear I'd end up skins. In the locker room and in slumber party settings, I was embarrassed to change in public. I didn't want to be made fun of.

I couldn't avoid it, however. I'm forty-seven years old at the time of this writing, and I still painfully remember coming to the breakfast table shirtless as a child and a family member making a joke about my chest. It put a deep shame beneath that impression. Another time, as a teenager, I didn't realize my brother had a friend over, and when I came down the stairs shirtless, it took that friend exactly two seconds to make fun of my chest.

These experiences taught me that I was absolutely right to hide, that I was ugly and unacceptable at the very time in life when feelings like that can really stick. When I got married, I was deathly afraid my wife would be repulsed and reject me.

I'm sure some reading this will think this is a lame thing to feel embarrassed about. And it probably is. All I know is, for years and years, I struggled with insecurity and anxiety and low self-esteem. Despite having quite a bit of outward achievement and ability, I also had this hidden deformity that prevented me from just freely living my life like I wanted to.

The problem with my chest is a real thing, but it's also a symbol, I guess. It's a symbol of the real me I don't want anyone to know or see. Here I am telling you about it, and I'm running the risk you'll think I'm a weirdo. But I'm also kind of hoping you'll be impressed by my transparency. See what a messed-up guy I am?

What I love about Jesus is that I can't play any of these games with him. He sees the angles I'm running. He knows the cards I keep close to the vest. And he knows what's behind the vest. I guess what I'm saying is, I can come to the breakfast table shirtless with Jesus.

I'm not saying I *would*. That'd be kind of weird. I'm just saying I *could*. And I wouldn't have to worry about a thing. He'd be neither impressed nor repulsed by me. Nor by you either, whatever your particular deformity, be it physical or otherwise, or any of the ways you try to cover it up.

Because of all the mess that is me, I tend to resonate most with the folks in the Bible who seem the messiest. I feel a kindred connection to the men and women who just hope to get by without anybody giving them too much trouble or even noticing them too much. I like the hiders.

I think of the woman with the bleeding issue in Mark 5. For twelve years, she's suffered from an apparently incurable condition. Even after spending all her money on doctors, her condition has only gotten worse. We don't know exactly what her infirmity is, but we know it's painful and embarrassing and basically cuts her off from society. Because of the constant flow of blood, she's considered unclean. If anybody could have a reason to just curl up in a corner and pray for death, it's this woman.

Even when she has the bright idea to look to Jesus for help, she cannot fathom the idea of his *wanting* to help her. Unlike Jairus, the important man who in the same chapter, in the same scene, goes directly to Jesus to look him in the eye and ask him to heal his daughter, this woman can only imagine her healing might come by stealth. She believes Jesus *can* heal her; she doesn't seem to believe he *will*. So she faces the disgust of the crowd to press in and through and feebly grab hold of the hem of Jesus's robe.

Perhaps the most important takeaway from this miraculous healing is this: you don't need a particularly mighty faith to receive the favor of God. Because it isn't the strength of the faith that saves but the strength of the Savior. If the faith is true, however small, it can lay hold of all the riches of grace in Christ Jesus.

As if to punctuate this point, Jesus turns to search out who, as it were, "stole" their healing. He finds that unclean woman staring back at him. She is embarrassed. Heck, she's *terrified*. And Jesus looks her in the eyes with that warm, intimidating gaze of his and calls her a name. But it's not like any of the choice words others, despising her and disgusted by her condition, have likely presented her with for years. No, the Holy One of Israel calls this unclean woman "daughter."

I think of the Samaritan woman in John 4, the one Jesus meets at Jacob's well. We can guess she's trying to be alone because of the time of day she goes to draw water. Most folks would attend the well in the cool of the morning or the cool of the evening. This woman goes during the hottest part of the day. Why? I assume because she's hiding.

Maybe she's tired of the sideways glares, the upturned noses, the gossipy whispers. Maybe she's tired of the outright judgment and insults. So she goes to a public place at the time she's least likely to be in the presence of others, and there's her new friend Jesus just standing there, waiting for her.

As they talk, she continues to hide behind theology and politics. But friendship is deeper than chitchat. He goes to the heart of the matter, revealing her hidden shame. But not to condemn her. To cover her.

We've been doing this hiding thing from the very beginning. We're all basically just Adam and Eve, lying low in the bushes (Gen. 3:7–8). But Jesus has been doing his seeking thing from the beginning. He comes walking after us, calling us to himself. We hide; he seeks.

And when we're found, it's usually covered in fig leaves.

Playing Pretend

One thing I love about Jesus is that everybody around knows he's hanging out with sinners. He isn't even trying to hide it. He doesn't care who sees. He doesn't care who knows. He doesn't even care that by spending time with "those people" he effectively is setting himself up to be judged as being one of those people himself.

Jesus shares table fellowship with the wrong kind of people. This is a really big deal. It's a much bigger deal, in fact, than a lot of folks make it out to be today. Some will say it's proof, for instance, that Jesus "likes to party," that he is cool with people doing whatever they want to do, that he just likes to have fun. This is an asinine reading of the relevant biblical texts, not simply because it makes Jesus out to be careless about sin but because it misses the real scandal, which is that Jesus both hates sin and is willing to be identified with sin in order to destroy it.

In 2 Corinthians 5:21, Paul writes, "He made the one who did not know sin to be sin for us, so that in him we might become the righteousness of God." What exactly does it mean that Jesus *became* sin? It doesn't mean that Jesus became a sinner. As the Son of God incarnate, our Savior was perfectly holy, utterly sinless. He was tempted as we are and experienced the frailty and hardship of humanity as we do, but because he was conceived by the Holy Spirit, he didn't have a sin nature or sinful passions. So for Jesus to "be sin" must mean something else.

I believe Jesus becoming sin derives from his closeness to sinners. He gets so close to the whores and the cheats and the drunkards that he's accused of their very sins. He's willing to bear the shame they bear, hear the insults they hear, feel the rejection they feel. Jesus is willing not just to preach to sinners but, risking his own reputation, to *be their friend*.

Indeed, Jesus isn't just willing to give up his reputation for sinners; he is willing to give up his life. Jesus becoming sin ultimately derives from this—that he willingly embraces the role of the sin *offering*, going to the cross to accept the due penalty of sin, the just wrath of God.

The friend of sinners takes the punishment sinners deserve as if he were the one deserving it. And the foe of sin takes the destruction sin deserves as if he were the one embodying it.

And the only people who seem not to appreciate this are those who don't see their sin as that big a deal. This includes the drunken sex fiend who lives for the weekend party scene and the deacon at the church around the corner who acts like that drunken sex fiend is beyond hope.

Among the religious and irreligious alike, the folks who don't seem to get what Jesus is doing—at least, not on a deep, heartfelt level—are those who don't think they're in all that much trouble without him. There are a lot of folks, for instance, who would no doubt profess that Jesus has identified with them, but this profession doesn't amount to much, because they themselves cannot identify with "those people." When we live our lives pretending we don't have all that much to forgive, pretending to be pretty put together or blaming our obvious lack of being put together on anybody and anything other than ourselves, the reality of friendship with God in Christ isn't all that spectacular a thing to us, because, well, who *wouldn't* want to be friends with us?

And what I love about Jesus's earthly friendships is how blatantly everybody knows who "those people" are. He attaches himself mainly to people who can't hide. Loose women and untrustworthy taxmen. Irascible fishermen and irredeemable street walkers. The unclean and the untouchable. The drunks and the skunks. That's who Jesus is constantly making friends with. He truly is a friend of sinners.

He would be friends with the religious elite, too, if they wanted it. The problem is, they're too busy playing pretend. They can't sit around a table with Jesus and let their guts hang over their bellies. They refuse to be seen as they truly are.

The truth is, the most religious Pharisee and the most educated scribe are neither any less nor any greater a sinner than the drunkard and the prostitute; it's just that not as many of them can make friends with Jesus because they can't admit that. The harder it is to hide, the easier it is, I suppose, to accept the gracious covering of Christ. But as long as we have religious garb, theological subterfuges, and doctrinal defenses to prop ourselves up and make ourselves look bigger than we actually are, we'll do that. We still like those fig leaves.

But you can be yourself with Jesus. He'll sit at the breakfast table with you whether you've got a shirt to put on or not. By his Spirit, he's committed to changing you, transforming you more and more into his own image, but he still loves you as you are in the moment. Remember: it's not the impressive version of you that he loves. He loves the real you.

Make Belief

The fact that Jesus will sit at a table with drunks and let unclean women anoint his feet means he can get close to you and me too. He has set the bar incredibly low. Anyone can qualify. He's accepting all applications. We just have to tell the truth. About ourselves and about him.

We have to start being honest about our own unworthiness. The minute we begin thinking we deserve friendship with Jesus is the minute we diminish our experience of it. We can put an obstacle between us and Jesus by believing we've merited his closeness.

The beautiful irony, however, is this: the more of a sinner we can admit ourselves to be, the closer our Savior can feel to us. The more we desire to rid ourselves of our sin, the closer our Savior will come to us. After all, as Christ himself said, "It is not those who are well who need a doctor, but those who are sick. I didn't come to call the righteous, but sinners" (Mark 2:17). It's not transparent confession that will repel him but religious pretense.

The more of yourself you are, the more of him you'll know. As deep as your need may be, Christ is deeper still. You will begin to see that for every ailment, he's the remedy. For every shame, he's the shelter. For every hunger, he's the true satisfaction. From every sin, he's the cleanser. But we can't have any of these precious gifts from Jesus if we can't admit we need them.

Come as you are to Christ Jesus. At his table of fellowship, no one has to play make-believe. In fact, the more real you are, the more by faith you open yourself to his grace, and the more he'll make the belief you need to trust him further. He will give more and more faith to the one whose starting point is just a mustard seed. He will strengthen the faith of the one who puts all their faith, frail as it may be, into his hands.

It doesn't matter what others think of you. It doesn't matter what they call you or if they've put you down, written you off, or thrown you out. Christ Jesus will stick by your side. This world might beat you up, but there's no friend so comforting as him.

And this is how close he's willing to get: "For the one who sanctifies and those who are sanctified all have one Father. That is why Jesus is not ashamed to call them brothers and sisters" (Heb. 2:11). The transformative closeness of God to the sinner isn't simply an association—it's an adoption!

Everything about us, from God's perspective, has changed. We submit our weak belief to him, and he shores it up with his goodness, building up our belief over time through our followship of his Son. Things with Jesus never get old. Familiarity doesn't breed contempt in the Christian walk. Rather, we experience newness the *more familiar* we become with him. The older we grow with Jesus, in fact, the newer we will be. As Paul says in 2 Corinthians 4:16, we might be falling apart outwardly, but "our inner person is being renewed day by day."

In fact, our identity—our very self—is changed by Jesus's closeness to us. Sinners now in Christ become saints. Strangers become friends. Orphans become children.

Through the gospel of grace, we sinners are declared holy, and the holy Father of the holy Christ becomes our Father too. By grace, through faith, we aren't simply recruited to the Lord's side as his friends but reconciled to him as family.

He calls us his brothers and sisters. And, friends, our big brother Jesus isn't ashamed to do this. He is, rightly understood, proud of us.

So let those away from the table sneer at us and call us sinners. Our precious Savior smiles at us. He says, "Don't pay any attention to them." He passes the bread. He listens to us. He laughs with us. When he speaks to us, his warmth is incomparable. His love is inscrutable. We've never felt such love, such acceptance, such encouragement as we do from him. When he addresses us, he calls us his friends, his brothers, his sisters. And there's nowhere in the world he'd rather be than with us.

We feel it. In his presence, playing pretend seems so stupid. Hiding seems pointless. At his table, we let our guard down. We let our hair down. We sigh. We breathe. We unsuck our gut. Because it's not the *idea* of us that he loves, but the *real* us—our dumb ole, foolish, real selves.

Now, isn't that a table you'd want to sit at for a long, long time?

5

Just Abide

(Jesus the Unhurried Friend)

The cure for too-much-to-do is solitude and silence, for there
you find you are safely more than what you do. And the cure
of loneliness is solitude and silence, for there you discover in
how many ways you are never alone.

Dallas Willard, *The Divine Conspiracy*[1]

There is no friend so unbothered as Jesus. He's not worried
or anxious. He never scrambles or hustles. Jesus doesn't
hurry. He lives in a constant state of unthreatened joy and
peace. Jesus just *is*.

And Jesus brings the glory of his self, the beauty of his
undistracted, undivided existence into his relationship with
us. He knows that our essential problem is that we fall short
of his glory (Rom. 3:23), so he brings the fullness of himself

to ensure that our closeness with him is as unhindered as possible, as *glorious* as possible. In fact, this is the end goal of the entire relationship, that we'd be sanctified according to his image until the day we're delivered before his very face, reflecting him perfectly glorified (Rom. 8:17; Col. 3:4). "We know that when he appears, we will be like him because we will see him as he is" (1 John 3:2).

Through friendship with Jesus, then, his beauty begins to beautify *us*.

While the process of sanctification necessarily entails good works that the indwelling Spirit performs through us, the working engine of our sanctification isn't our obedience but Christ dwelling in our hearts through faith. The same grace that saved us is saving us. The same gospel that empowered our justification is now empowering our sanctification. And the whole point of this sanctification isn't that we're trading in bad behavior for good behavior but that we're trading in our sinful hearts for the pure heart of Christ.

To become more like Jesus is the point. But we can't become like anyone with whom we don't spend any time. So he draws us to himself. He invites us into his unbothered, undistracted presence.

We cannot perfectly replicate his lack of division, his lack of compartmentalization. We cannot replicate his focus. But we can enjoy it, be changed by it, and see more of these things manifest in our own lives as we work through the awkward silences in his presence to engage the divine dialogue and, honestly, sometimes just stare at him. The more we behold Jesus, the more we become like him (2 Cor. 3:18).

There's a storm inside of us for which he is the peace. This peace comes to us from his very self. Indeed, Paul tells us that Jesus is our peace (Eph. 2:14). And Jesus tells us that he wants to give this peace to us (John 14:27). He says that he doesn't give as the world gives. The world gives with strings attached and breaks promises. Our Lord Jesus gives himself fully and freely to those he loves, and the effect is a peace that surpasses our understanding (Phil. 4:7).

Being in the presence of Jesus is a transformative thing, even in the minutest of details. Sense Jesus's posture—unguarded, unanxious, open. Sense Jesus's countenance—warm, gentle, calm. See in your mind's eye how wholly committed he is to you. The fact that he's instantaneously available to all who desire his presence at any given moment in the day isn't a challenge for him at all. Jesus is the friend who doesn't check his watch while you're talking to him.

His presence is affectionate and faithful. He lingers, he dwells, he tarries. This is good news for us, because the deep heart work we need to make life worth living, to get all that we can out of it, is contingent upon a measured slowness and intentionality. Deep heart work from the Spirit requires deep dwelling with Jesus, a slow plodding with him. And he is always up for it.

I have a friend named Michael who is one of the slowest moving people I've ever known. We met working at a bookstore together. We worked in the same department, and while I was always rushing around, feeding my anxiety with constant tasks and expectations from customers, Michael was always taking his sweet time doing anything and everything. It was supremely frustrating. Until I realized why.

I didn't get it at the time, but Michael's slowness irritated me because it convicted me. He was not only slow, he was always pleasant. He had a joy that was unshakable. You couldn't rattle him. You couldn't get him to lose his temper. You couldn't get him to feel flustered. Maybe I'm just making assumptions, and he did feel all those things internally, but he certainly never showed them. And I think his innate ability to work and relate in a committedly unhurried way fed his innate pleasantness. All these years later, I still marvel at his peacefulness, but I'm no longer irritated by it. I'm jealous of it, in fact.

Most of us have trouble with being still. Our culture is built on anxiety. And all the technological advancements and emphasis on self-care in the world haven't solved our addiction to work. In fact, now we valorize not just works righteousness but "workaholism righteousness." We champion the grind, the hustle. We imagine that we're sanctified by our success, that we *are* our accomplishments.

In a severe mercy, then, God will often come along and disrupt the whole frenzied enterprise. He will bring us low to make us slow. He will crush us.

Even the oft-quoted Psalm 46:10 is about this. "Be still and know that I am God," many translations of the verse begin. The impression is one of embracing calm, perhaps of "letting go and letting God." The CSB renders the verse "Stop fighting, and know that I am God." This is closer to the contextual meaning. Through the psalmist's poetic language, God is interrupting a godless striving with an arresting vision of his glory. The surrounding verses are about God's judgment, about the devastation he brings to the earth. Psalm 46:10, then, is less about taking a load off by a gentle stream as you have your morning devotional and more about God grabbing hold of careless strivers and squeezing them until they pass out.

He wants us to just abide in his glorious presence so much that he's willing to knock our legs out from under us. So often the Lord crushes individuals to make them still. But it's okay. He was willing to be crushed too.

Taking a Load Off

I don't think of myself as an overworker. I like to relax. A lot. I try to take time out of each day to do nothing. And I especially enjoy whole days of doing nothing. I think I naturally tend toward laziness. I procrastinate. It takes me a while even once I've started a task to focus on it. But when I look at my calendar and consider the number of hats I wear in my work life, I'm not sure I'm as lazy as I think I am. In fact, my body often reminds me that my pace of life isn't as leisurely as I sometimes fear it is.

A couple of years ago, before a speaking engagement, I suffered an anxiety attack and ended up spending a week in and out of doctor's offices trying to figure out what was wrong with me. At the time, I thought I was having a heart attack. I'd never experienced anything like it, though a few years prior I'd begun suffering from a strange driving anxiety that regularly kept me off busy highways or off the streets in general in bad weather. Still, I'd never experienced the sensation of my whole body shutting down. Sitting in my office, not doing much of anything, just waiting for my turn to speak at our annual student conference, I felt like I was about to die.

The doctor told me to give up caffeine. That was pretty easy to do. She also told me I needed to cut back on my pace of life. I thought to myself, *But I don't do that much.*

However, my body thought otherwise. It had picked a point at which it seemed okay to fall apart on me. It was telling me I had limits.

I teach and I write. I coach and I disciple. I travel a lot to speak and to preach. Recently I added pastoring back into the mix, as our church has installed me as a lay elder.

Am I an idiot?

Yes.

As I try to diagnose my major malfunctions, I come to face a couple realities of my personality. First, while I may not work the same hours every day that a lot of workaholics do, when I'm working, it's hard for me to pause, to breathe, to find a sustainable pace. When I'm focused, I'm all in. Second, I'm a terrible multitasker. It's difficult for me to think about multiple things at once, much less do multiple things at once. This has some benefits for focused work. But it also means that the fact I maintain multiple jobs and roles is a constant source of stress and anxiety for me. I frequently feel as though I'm working in the redline.

Now, I'm not prepared to give up any of my roles. In fact, I do believe I'm running in the lanes to which God has called me. But it means that I have to constantly remember one of the lanes to which he's called me is on the sideline. And if I won't regularly take a time-out to sit on the bench, drink some water, and catch my breath, he'll tackle me as I'm running and carry me there.

I think another reason I'm prone to redline working is that I feel very guilty about the prolonged season of laziness I had in my early twenties. In a way, I'm still trying to make up for all the time I wasted back then. It's my own weird repentance tour. If I can get four times as much done in my forties, maybe God won't be as disappointed in me as I imagine he was in my twenties.

Throughout my childhood and into my teenage years, my discipleship training largely consisted of Bible knowledge and doing things for Jesus. I got pretty good at the Bible stuff. It was the "doing things" that tripped me up. I never felt like I could do enough. My own internal fears and insecurities were working against me. I never measured up, and back then my whole conception of my relationship with God was built upon the idea of measuring up.

So here's what I did: I got reasonably good at pretending I was a good Christian kid so that others would approve of me, while in reality I'd pretty much given up trying to please God because I didn't think it was possible. The result was a public appearance of religiosity with a private disconnect with Christ. And that's how I lived for a long time. I became outwardly performative while privately lazy. I wasn't really trying to abide with Christ. I didn't think I could, and I wasn't sure he wanted me to.

Then God tackled me. In my late twenties, when my hidden sin exploded into the open and blew up my world, God upended my life. He ruined me. I got exposed to those who mattered most as a total fraud. Everything got torn up. I went from lazy to *low*. I went from unwilling to work to, in a way, *unable* to. And it was the best thing that could've happened to me.

While I spent nearly a year scraping the bottom of the barrel, feeling nothing but my own bankruptcy and brokenness, I had no choice but to call out to God. If you've ever been through a profound season of suffering, you probably know exactly what I'm talking about. When you're at the end of your rope, you just pray differently. And when you don't know how to pray at all, still somehow you sense the Spirit doing it for you. I truly believe that for a great many of us, God won't become our only hope until God *is* our only hope.

In those days of hurt and lowness, my assumptions about discipleship were rearranged. Like Isaiah in the temple, I'd been utterly ruined, I was crying out "Woe is me!" The process of being put back together burned in a lot of ways, but I was also being changed. The closeness of Christ can be a discombobulating thing, but it's also a renewing thing. I was being reconstituted, reconstructed. And I came out of it with an entirely new awareness of the gospel's power for even stupid believers like me.

I discovered through this painful, wonderful process that Christ wasn't just my justification at my conversion but every minute after it forever after. And I experienced a renewing power in having been completely flattened that I never experienced in all my days of self-righteously "doing things" for Jesus.

Christ made me small that he might be big.

Sitting a Spell

This is really what I'm getting at with the whole servant spirituality versus friendship spirituality thing. A friendship spirituality is one in which we understand that Christ's disposition toward us isn't as a taskmaster demanding we perform for him but as a good older brother who cares for us and as a best friend who requests mostly from us that we just come and sit a spell.

Do you remember that scene from Luke's Gospel when Jesus visits his friends Mary and Martha?

> While they were traveling, he entered a village, and a woman named Martha welcomed him into her home. She had a sister named Mary, who also sat at the Lord's feet and was listening to what he said. But Martha was distracted by her many tasks, and she came up and asked, "Lord, don't you care that my sister has left me to serve alone? So tell her to give me a hand."
>
> The Lord answered her, "Martha, Martha, you are worried and upset about many things, but one thing is necessary. Mary has made the right choice, and it will not be taken away from her." (10:38–42)

Martha gets a bad rap, I think. She's simply trying to be a good host. It's her home, after all. But she grows a little resentful that she's having to work so hard to get everything *just so* for Jesus while Mary just sits there with Jesus.

We can see that Martha's heart isn't in the right place for two reasons. One, she's distracted by these tasks. She's not doing anything wrong per se; it's only that she has chosen "doing things" *for* Jesus over just being *with* Jesus. She's relating to her friend through servant spirituality. Two, she's comparing herself to Mary and judging herself as righteous. In Martha's eyes, Mary is being lazy. *Why should I have to work if she's not going to work?* she's thinking. *Surely Jesus recognizes I'm winning the Christianity game at this moment.* So she tells Jesus to *command* Mary. She wants Mary neck-deep in servant spirituality with her.

Perhaps to her surprise, Jesus flips the script. "No, the one necessary task," he says, "is to abide with me."

To sit at the feet of Jesus is the highest and best experience we can have. He knows we need to change. He knows we need to produce good fruit and perform good works. But he also knows that none of that matters—or can truly even happen—if we don't make it a priority to sit still with him and listen.

Some friends it's hard work to be around. But not Jesus. Christian, he truly is inviting you to pull up a chair and take a load off. "Come to me," he says, "all of you who are weary and burdened, and I will give you rest" (Matt. 11:28).

Embracing the Inefficiency

I once heard pastor and author John Piper say, "I thought I'd be more sanctified by now." The statement took me aback, because if you know anything about Piper, it's that he's intensely serious about holiness. He's a very sober man, well known for his sacrificial frugality, his "wartime lifestyle," and his wholehearted commitment to ultimate satisfaction in God alone. If I could point at one public figure in our evangelical culture as exemplifying sanctification, I'd probably point at John Piper. And yet in a moment of humble transparency, he admitted he'd expected to be further along in his spiritual growth at his age.

On one level, this confession terrifies me. It makes me think, *If John Piper isn't sanctified, what hope do I have?* But on another level, I find it incredibly encouraging. Because if a mature and godly leader like John Piper senses his own lack of sanctification, it means I might *at the very least* be normal to wonder about my own.

I thought I'd be a lot more sanctified in my middle-aged years. Now, I can definitely see, by God's grace, that I'm not what I was! But I also know I'm not what I ought to be. The Lord has done a lot of work in me, and I can honestly point to past struggles, especially with certain sins, that aren't quite so troubling for me anymore. I've experienced notable victories in numerous areas of my life. Every person who has walked with Christ for even a little bit of time should be able to identify such growth in their life. But I still tremble about all the ground I've yet to make up. I still at various times find this journey I'm on with Christ to be frustrating.

If I hadn't learned this in my own spiritual walk, I would certainly have learned it from the work of pastoral ministry—discipleship is frustratingly inefficient. Every week I'd preach, I was burdened by all the brokenness in the congregation, by all the sins of my people I was aware of (and all the sins I wasn't), and yet I kept plugging along, hoping a weekly exposure to a word from God would inspire more of them to get their act together. In the counseling room, I'd ache in the knowledge that most people struggled with the same sins and worries for a long time. I had no silver bullets. I had no magic incantations. As soon as we had conquered one area, two more would need our attention, and while we focused on those, that first area had fallen back into neglect.

Broken people are people of broken habits. We get into ruts. Our sins become besetting. And it's hard, if not impossible, to walk in victory as we imagine.

From my early days of equating spiritual growth with a "chore chart" mentality and "doing things for Jesus" to my later, more mature years of just lamenting the stupid habits and sinful tendencies I can't seem to shake, I know that following Jesus is as much about failure as about success, if not more so.

In a lot of ways, the Christian life can feel like a big spiritual version of Whac-A-Mole. As soon as I've beaten one messy thing out of my life, two more need my attention. Christian discipleship feels a lot like trying to empty Lake Michigan by bailing it with a shot glass. I'm doing a lot of work. But I'm no closer to being done than when I started. Is it even worth it?

The apostle Paul seems to get at this irritating dynamic in Romans 7 when he talks about how he finds himself doing the things he knows he shouldn't and not doing the things he knows he should. Shouldn't Paul be more sanctified?

To the modern mind, in which convenience and comfortability are sacred virtues, inefficiency is proof that something *doesn't work*, or at the very least isn't worth it. To the self-righteous mind, inefficiency is proof no real growth is happening.

Pastors set on efficiency as a means of evident success move their congregants through a succession of "discipleship training" classes and other church programs to be able to pat themselves on the back about the growth being experienced. They set measurable goals for attendance and giving and then tailor the experience of their churches in such a way as to maximize the opportunity to meet those goals. And all along, their people may not be growing in any substantive ways at all—not in the ways that count. What kind of classroom training, after all, can evaluate the character of the students? We can test people's theological knowledge in a classroom setting, and we can visibly count attendance and tithes, but how do we know people are growing spiritually?

Spiritual growth is harder to measure. It's much less efficient.

I have learned, however, that experiencing inefficiency in the Christian life is a huge part of the point! For one thing, reckoning rightly with our propensity for failure puts us in touch with our inherent neediness, which is an essential component of intimacy with Christ. If our spiritual walk was one of ever-increasing ease, how would we increasingly sense our need for Jesus?

Instead, the more we walk with Jesus and the closer we get to him, the more deficiencies we see in ourselves—as increasing closeness to his light increases the illumination of the hidden things in us. The closer to Christ we come, the more of our true selves we see in the light of his holiness. Because of this, in many ways, an increasing sense of inefficiency can be a sign of growing maturity! People far from God tend to care less about their sanctification unto holiness. The easiest thing in the world is for sinners to live apart from God. It is our natural bent. It is our natural way of "going with the flow."

Therefore, maturing Christians come not to begrudge the inefficiency of discipleship but to embrace it. We know that the very lament of not being further along is itself a sign of the Spirit's working in us. The conviction we feel about our sin is a sign of his closeness. The pain we feel in our battle with the flesh is a sign of bearing Christ's cross.

You cannot get close to Jesus without touching his wounds.

Our Savior says, "Take up my yoke and learn from me," and we feel that yoke around our necks. And yet he adds, "For my yoke is easy and my burden is light" (Matt. 11:29–30).

How can this be so?

Jesus explains, "Because I am lowly and humble in heart" (v. 29).

The inefficiency of discipleship is an opportunity to rest. Not to rest from obedience. Not to rest from worship. But to rest *in him*.

To take Christ's yoke upon ourselves isn't a call to give up but to give up thinking everything depends on us. The latter is the yoke of legalism. It's the burden of self-righteousness. That burden is one of *never enough*. It's exhausting and only leads to devastation. Taking Christ's easy yoke and light burden, however, is embracing his finished work as our validation and approval. It's our resting in justification by grace alone through faith alone in Christ alone. When we screw up and fall down, we can throw ourselves back into his loving arms, because he has accomplished all we need to survive.

What I'm saying is, when Jesus declares from the cross, "It is finished" (John 19:30), he means it.

Because all the work we need to be fully justified by God was accomplished by Christ on the cross and out of that empty tomb, we need not fear the frustrations of spiritual growth. We can know that he will finish the work he began (Phil. 1:6). He will see us through, even when we can't see through the weeds. He will deliver us safe, even though we're teetering over a treacherous ravine.

The gospel of Jesus Christ promises us his commitment to us for eternity. We can embrace the inefficiency of our spiritual growth, because we know God has the big picture perspective. We ought to share this long view with him.

As we walk the narrow road with Jesus, we discover it's not a perfectly upward trajectory. It's less like walking up a hill and more like hiking up a mountain. We may experience frustrating setbacks, confusing switchbacks, and overfilled backpacks. But the whole journey is changing us and is being used toward our good and his glory. He will make sure of it.

He just wants us to stick close.

Embrace the inefficiency, and you'll find plenty of occasions to sit at the feet of Jesus. Perhaps busyness isn't the point. Maybe it's not always about doing something but rather just sitting there. Especially if we're trying to run far ahead of where he's working in and through us.

His yoke is easy, and his burden is light. He's not calling us to religious busywork on his behalf. He's calling us to abide. That's hard to do if our minds are always set on getting things done.

And there is a wonderful paradox in this. The more intentionally we embrace the stillness of Christ's presence, the more effectively will we glorify him.

"Remain in me, and I in you," he says. "Just as a branch is unable to produce fruit by itself unless it remains on the vine, neither can you unless you remain in me" (John 15:4). Fruitfulness, it turns out, is the result of an unhurried abiding with Christ.

Hanging Around the House

I find it lovely how often in the Gospels Jesus is still. He's allotted only three short and ministry-heavy years to proclaim the coming of the kingdom of God in and through himself. This work is set to culminate in his single-minded dedication to the cross. And yet so often he's just *hanging out*.

He naps. He withdraws to desolate places to be alone. (Luke 5:16 tells us he does this often.) He spends a lot of time sharing meals and going to parties. He takes time to entertain kids. It turns out that Jesus is a great hang.

Jesus does all of this with a great purpose. He wants to draw us into the joy and peace of his own life. His Father is creating a big family, a community of blood-bought brothers and sisters who will be brought into his security and under his favor to bask in his presence, and Jesus is wooing us to join in.

Some of my fondest memories of friendship when I was a teenager don't have anything to do with exploits on the football field or basketball court, high marks in a favorite class, or doing anything intentional. They have more to do with the times my buddies and I were just giving each other a hard time sitting in somebody's living room or riding around in somebody's car.

When you were younger, wasn't there one house all of your friends gravitated toward? Maybe because there was a swimming pool or a Ping-Pong table. Maybe because it had comfy couches. Maybe Mom was extra welcoming and cheerfully hospitable and Dad was funny and easygoing. Maybe there were plenty of snacks, plenty of things to do, and usually a comfortable place to chill out and cut up when you didn't want to do anything. But the real draw was probably because you and your friends just felt most at home there. You could relax, be yourself, and never feel like you were wearing out your welcome.

I've realized in my older years that, for some of my friends, being at someone else's house might have felt more like being home than their own houses. When you're a kid, you don't quite know what's going on in the homes you never visit. Sometimes you get a glimpse, though. Unclean living spaces.

Bickering or overbearing parents. Maybe abusive parents. For these kids, another friend's home of welcome becomes a respite for them, even a taste of heaven. *This is what it could be like*, they think. *This is what I've been missing.*

My wife is the most gifted hostess I've ever known. Her heart is full when our home is full. We throw a lot of parties and house our share of visitors. And even though I'm a raging introvert who finds most social situations overwhelming, I love sitting around our firepit with fifteen of our friends, just talking about *whatever*.

The gift of hospitality referenced in the Scriptures is a nod to this. Of course, biblical hospitality isn't about hosting friends and family but strangers and aliens. God commends this kind of hospitality as an expression of evangelism and as an expression of his own heart toward sinners. Before Christ comes into our lives, we are strangers and aliens to the household of God. But he seeks us out, invites us in, and gives us full rights to the run of the place, as if we are his Son's own flesh and blood (Eph. 2:19). Our heavenly Father isn't seeking sinners to populate his house like servant-orphans but to live like adopted children, co-heirs with Jesus of all his promises.

David famously sings,

> I have asked one thing from the LORD;
> it is what I desire:
> to dwell in the house of the LORD
> all the days of my life. (Ps. 27:4)

This man is in a time of great trouble. One day he will be king, and he will have the most lavish mansion in all the land. But he's not looking to that here. In this prayerful song, he says he wants nothing more than to just abide in God's house.

We often interpret this reference today as a commendation of church services. And certainly it's a high privilege and wonderful blessing to join God's people in exalting him on Sunday morning. But that's not exactly what David is getting at here. He's speaking to the larger reality of being *at home* with God. This has implications for corporate worship, sure. And he's making a far-reaching nod to living in heaven forever when he dies. But as he references the temple at the end of that verse, we know David is referencing a more immediate reality. He desires now to be swallowed up in the presence of God. "All the days of my life," he says. Doing what? "Gazing on the beauty of the LORD" (v. 4).

David just wants to be at home with God.

Don't you?

The good news is that Jesus has come to make his home among us. "The Word became flesh and dwelt among us" (John 1:14). The word *dwelt* in this verse literally means "dwelt in a tent." The Lord of heaven didn't wait for us to figure out how to climb up to him. He came to us and set up house. And even though he has ascended from whence he came, he assures us he's not going to leave us homeless.

> In my Father's house are many rooms. If it were not so, would I have told you that I am going to prepare a place for you? If I go away and prepare a place for you, I will come again and take you to myself, so that where I am you may be also. (14:2–3)

He's made mansions for us. He's getting them all ready, so when the time comes to draw us up to himself into the everlasting bliss of paradise, we'll have the best hang ever.

Because Jesus promises that he's making all things new (as opposed to all new *things*), I imagine after his return, the new earth will have some continuity with the old earth. It won't be the same; it will be renewed, restored. Sin will be vanquished; grief will be gone. All the brokenness and the curse of this side of the veil will be forever cured. But I suppose there will still be something like work in the world to come. If there is work in the new heavens and new earth, it won't hurt and it won't be frustrating. I imagine it will be unimaginably fruitful.

I don't know how work in heaven will, well, *work*, but I do know the one thing Jesus has said he's going ahead of us to make is a house. Which means, work or not, we're looking forward to a glorious day of never-ending rest. We're looking forward to dwelling with him, gazing at his beauty. We're looking forward to an eternity of simply *being with Jesus*.

We can taste some of this heavenly reality now, bring a bit of it to earth to enjoy today, when we sit at his feet, enjoy his presence, and devote our hearts to knowing what it means to dwell with him in his house.

If we will make just abiding with Jesus part of our daily routine, it'll change us in ways we can't fully comprehend. Just like sitting around the firepit or lounging in the living room with buddies, even if the conversation is superficial, speaks to a deep part of our hearts of something settling and soothing, daily sitting with Jesus and engaging with him in the divine dialogue of Scripture meditation and prayer will profoundly impact our souls.

The homes we grow up in shape us in ways that are sometimes imperceptible. Whether our homelife was healthy or broken, it affects us for a long, long time. Any place in which we spend most of our time for days on end will rub off on us. Our environments steer our values, our expectations, our appetites. Urban environments may stoke our busyness and anxiety but also our productivity and ambition. Suburban environments may serve our desires for convenience and comfort but also for community and family. Rural environments may make us slower and more naïve but also more patient and more resilient.

Wherever we live is making us who we are. Thus it is with the presence of God. He has tabernacled among us, and he invites us in to rest with him. The idea may be strange to our fleshly senses and odd to our worldly sensibilities, but our insidest insides know we were made for this. We were made to know God like this.

Now, after the fall, because of the infection of sin, all our wiring has been crossed. So you and I are constantly seeking out the wrong ways to feel the kind of stability we spiritually crave. But when we truly abide in Christ, we come to realize we've finally come home.

Our friend Jesus is in heaven preparing a room for us. The question is, Are we here preparing room for him?

6

The Law against Double Jeopardy

(Jesus the Loyal Friend)

[Our sins] are now cast into the deepest sea and a sign is put up that says No Fishing Allowed.

Corrie ten Boom, *Tramp for the Lord*[1]

There is no friend more loyal than Jesus. He will always stick by you. He will always stick up for you. He has pledged allegiance to you. Through thick and thin, come hell or high water, he will be your eager and able defense.

Jesus is more than able, in fact, to defend each of us against the onslaught of all tyranny, the barrage of all accusations, the promise of all threats. Hebrews 7:25 tells us "he is able to save completely those who come to God through him, since he always lives to intercede for them." He makes it his living to intercede for us. He defends us like it's his job. And Jesus is the guy who always does his job. Everybody else is the other guy.

There's another scene with Jesus's friends Mary and Martha that illustrates his defense perfectly. In John 12:1–7, the Lord is at their home again, having a meal with Lazarus (the fellow he previously raised from the dead). Martha is, of course, serving, and Mary is back at Jesus's feet, this time with a very expensive jar of perfume. She pours it over his feet and wipes it with her hair. (I know, it sounds kind of weird.) One of his disciples objects—not to that part but rather to the apparent "wasting" of the perfume.

Naturally, the objector is Judas, who has always been obsessed with money, which will eventually lead him to betraying the Savior. He tries to make his indignation sound noble. If we're going to waste perfume, he argues, we could have just sold it and given the money to the poor.

Jesus, though, understands Mary is doing a burial anointing. Whether she intends this or not, he receives it as a preparation for his coming death. And I love what he says to Judas in verse 7: "Leave her alone."

He says more than that, obviously, but that first part I just find delicious. Even when I'm fumbling about my spiritual walk, with all my flaws and frailty, the Lord says to my accusers: "Leave him alone."

Perhaps the closest we come in Jesus's ministry to a courtroom scene, apart from his own shoddy trials after his betrayal and arrest, is the moment in John 8 where Jesus receives the woman caught in adultery.[2] Jesus is teaching in the temple, doing what he always does, which is declaring himself as the culmination of and authority over the old covenant. The religious leaders drag this woman before him, intending to execute her, which by Jewish law is the appropriate punishment for her sin. The account tells us that this whole thing is a farce meant to trap Jesus in some kind of religious violation.

Then Jesus does something curious. He begins writing in the dirt. The text doesn't say what he's writing. (Perhaps that's one indication this is based on an eyewitness account.) Some think he's writing out details from the law, things that would in fact condemn many of those standing around, stones in hand, ready to kill. Maybe he's writing their names, showing he knows everything about them. Some think maybe he's listing all of their sins. I wonder if he's not just doodling, showing how unthreatened he is by this murderous setup.

Standing in the center of the temple, Jesus shows everyone he owns the room. He basically tells them, "Okay, you can kill her . . . if you don't have any sins of your own."

And they all slink away.

The story tells us that the older men left first, and I confess I'm not sure what to make of that. Is it because the older we are, the more sins we've accumulated? Is it because there's more wisdom with age, hidden though it may be sometimes by our anger and irrationality? Maybe it's because younger people have more energy and zeal for their "righteous causes." Whatever the case, in the end it's just Jesus and the woman standing alone.

And he doesn't say to her, "Well, I'm the only man here without sin, so I'll be the one to execute you." No, in a startling plot twist, he says, "Neither do I condemn you" (v. 11).

He acknowledges that she's a sinner, certainly. Jesus will never tell us we're something we're not. (More on that in the next chapter.) He commands her to a life of repentance. But Jesus is telling her—and us—that a life of repentance comes most powerfully from a heart that's been set free.

It's hard to repent if you know you can't avoid condemnation anyway.

Jesus is the great Judge. He is an uncorruptible juror. And he has every right to serve as executioner. No one is worthy to fill these roles but Jesus. And standing in the supreme court of the weightiest matters of heaven and earth, he issues his ruling to those who claim his mercy: "I don't condemn you."

In Romans 8:1, Paul turns this reality into a gospel declaration: "Therefore, there is now no condemnation for those in Christ Jesus." Notice Paul doesn't say, "There *was* no condemnation," as if receiving salvation is some kind of one time Get Out of Jail Free card. No, he says, "There is *now* no condemnation," present tense.

This is the ongoing verdict invisibly following every follower of Jesus. We are justified forever. No Christian is in danger of condemnation, ever. Jesus is always living to intercede for us.

A Ready Defense

Several years ago a former friend contacted my pastor, ostensibly to see if I could be put under church discipline. This fellow had sinned against me numerous times, and in my efforts to address the matter with him, he proved unable to admit any wrongdoing. He said he wanted to reconcile with me, but it's hard to reconcile with a person who's wronged you if they won't apologize for the wrong, won't stop doing the wrong, and in fact won't even admit what they're doing is wrong. So I told him I forgave him but we couldn't have a friendly relationship, and I moved on.

That wasn't good enough for him, however, and after I was unreceptive to his subsequent attempts to manipulate me, he messaged my pastor to get me in trouble.

Now, I have to hand it to my pastor. He didn't know this guy. But he knew me. And he could have easily just blown it off. Instead, he brought the concern to me. He said, "Here is what this fellow is alleging. Before I respond, can you answer for this?" So I did. I showed him all of the correspondence with my accuser, all of our exchanges, demonstrating at numerous points that he had even the basic facts of the complaint wrong. He'd told my pastor I had done things I hadn't and hadn't done things I had. I was able to set the record straight.

Because it really didn't matter how this guy felt or how I felt. What mattered was the truth of the situation. And as I sadly recounted the history of this falling out with my former friend, I had all the evidence necessary to make the case for my innocence in the matter, as well as the evidence for his guilt. In other words, unlike my accuser, I didn't just have accusations, I had proof.

You and I swim in a sea of accusation. It may not usually come from ex-friends who have turned on us. Normally it's just the ambient temperature of living in a culture opposed to the way of God. You don't have to do anything special—just be a Christian minding your own business, and you will learn that you are a bigot, a hypocrite, a narrow-minded believer in fairy tales. You will be told that you hate people you simply disagree with, even if you're not actively disagreeing with them. Even if you never said anything remotely judgmental to them, when someone committed to a way of life in rebellion against biblical standards somehow discovers you're a Christian, they will feel betrayed by you and lied to by you.

Those who do regularly take stands for biblical truth, who wear their Christianity on their shirtsleeves, have it even worse. These days, the accusations roll in with greater frequency and greater intensity.

But even if we've managed to somehow avoid all that (staying off social media helps), no Christian can avoid the voice of the accuser. The hiss of our enemy is always in our ear, tempting us and trying us. He will tell us we are not loved. He will tell us we can't be saved. He will tell us we're sorry excuses for children of God.

Sometimes this voice mixes in a little bit of truth with his lies. But even when he's telling the truth, he doesn't tell the *whole* truth. He uses it, positions it, twists it *just enough* to frame it in the way of condemnation.

When we hear the voice of condemnation, we have to be very careful. Because what our flesh yearns to do is either cower in despair or puff up in false bravado. If we believe the accuser, we will fall prey to his desire to hurt us and render us joyless and ineffective for God's kingdom. But even if we disbelieve him, we must be cautious. Many have tried to overcome the accuser's words with words of their own. When the devil tells us we're horrible sinners, we tell ourselves we're good. When the devil questions God's love for us, we tell ourselves we deserve that love. When the devil attacks the self, we exalt the self. But the voice of the accuser won't be adequately silenced by words of self-esteem.

You cannot fight how the devil feels about you with how *you* feel about you. Even if you feel pretty darn good about yourself. No, you need a stronger defense. You need a ready defense. You don't need feelings the accusations are wrong; you need proof!

And the only real evidence of our innocence in the judgment of God is the blood shed for us on the cross. Jesus Christ's willing substitution for us in absorbing the wrath we deserve and dying the death we owed is our only hope. Not only will the gospel of Christ's cross disprove the accuser; it will silence him.

If you're a defendant in a courtroom, you need facts on your side. You need the evidence to go your way. Oh, the experts will tell you that defendants don't have to prove anything, that the burden of proof is on the prosecution. But when the prosecution starts making charges, the effect is still weighty even if they offer only scanty proof or even no proof. How will you respond? How will you fight spurious charges? What can you place before a judge or jury to demonstrate that you should be found not guilty?

Imagine you're accused of murder. You didn't do it, of course, but the case seems pretty strong. The accusations come from some very cunning people. Their words are powerful. They seem to be swaying the court's opinion. Now, imagine somehow your defense has gotten hold of real, tangible evidence that someone else committed this murder. Maybe there's some DNA test that's inconvenient to the prosecutor. Maybe there's video or photographic evidence. That would be proof, wouldn't it, that someone else had done what you're accused of doing?

So when our accuser comes along and tells us we stand condemned, tells us God is punishing us or will punish us, instead of arguing with him based on how we feel, we point to the historic record of the cross. We direct his attention to the geographic place of Mount Calvary. We slam down on the table in front of him the promise of Romans 8:1. These are all proof that we couldn't possibly be in the place of condemnation; someone else was there instead. Christ our substitute was found guilty that we might be treated, according to the Judge's eyes, innocent.

The cross of Jesus is eternal exculpatory evidence for the sinner who trusts in him.

If you don't know what *exculpatory* means, you probably don't love true-crime shows and crime movies like my wife and I do. We especially love the stories, fiction or nonfiction, where there's a huge twist. Somebody presumed innocent is proven guilty, or vice versa, by a surprise piece of evidence or witness. Something exciting happens at just the right moment to upend the entire case, and everything we thought we knew has to be reevaluated and reconsidered.

This is kind of like what happens in the legal proceedings of the gospel. In the divine courtroom, the evidence for our being a sinner is great. It's practically insurmountable. The case, as they say, is airtight. We are definitely guilty.

But then there's a shocking twist! A surprise witness comes forward, the man Jesus Christ. He stands before the Judge and invites the verdict upon himself. He desires our acquittal and his own conviction in our place. Our condemnation effectively becomes his condemnation, thus rendering justice totally satisfied. Justice somehow isn't perverted, because someone *is* paying for our crime. It's just not us.

I know it doesn't work that way in earthly courts, but aren't you glad it does in the heavenly court? The Son of God serves not just as our Judge but as our defense attorney, pleading his own work on our behalf. He serves as our proxy, standing in our place to receive our verdict upon himself, so that justice might be done and we might at the same time be set free.

But it's not just the accusations from the outside to which the Lord puts an end.

The Charges Are Dropped

I was in Detroit, Michigan, a few years back, preaching at a pastors' event in a relatively new church plant located in a very impoverished area of the city. The neighborhood looked like what a lot of people sadly picture when they imagine a Detroit neighborhood. Lots of abandoned homes were in devastating states of disrepair. Tall weeds filled the green spaces, which were ornamented with all kinds of litter and detritus. It was a high crime area impacted by the drug epidemic. And smack dab in the middle of all this need stood a little outpost of grace, which had set up shop in a vacant post office.

On a big wall in the back of the church building, someone had painted a colorful mural in urban graphic style. In big graffiti letters, a declaration was emblazoned over the mural, impossible not to notice. It read, ALL THE CHARGES AGAINST ME HAVE BEEN DROPPED.

I've thought about that statement—about that specific wording—every few months since then. I'm not sure why, but I haven't been able to shake it. Using language that might resonate in a neighborhood with inordinately high rates of incarceration, it's a vivid and personal reminder of the surprising divine justice of the gospel.

See, when our great Judge renders his verdict about us as not guilty, based on the evidence of Christ's satisfaction of what we owe him, the charges against us become null and void. In essence, there isn't even a trial. Jesus takes our place in the seat of the accused, and the charges against us are dropped.

The good news of Christ's sinless life, sacrificial death, and glorious resurrection means it's not simply that the satanic accuser is silenced; it also means that the one we should really fear, the one who can't only destroy our body but also destroy our soul, doesn't accuse us either. It isn't the devil, after all, to whom we must give an account. It isn't the devil whose glory we've fallen short of. No, the standard we fall guilty against is the holiness of the almighty God. And yet he stands over us to say, in perpetuity, "Neither do I condemn you."

We have ample biblical evidence for this stunning development. Consider Ephesians 5:27, where Paul writes, "He did this to present the church to himself in splendor, without spot or wrinkle or anything like that, but holy and blameless." The apostle echoes that announcement in Colossians 1:22: "But now he has reconciled you by his physical body through his death, to present you holy, faultless, and blameless before him."

The word "blameless" is doing a lot of heavy lifting here. (Actually, it's Jesus who is doing the heavy lifting.) *Blameless* is a staggering adjective for the church, when we really think

125

about it. We know we're sinners. God knows better than we do that we're sinners! And yet he has committed himself, through the sending of his Son, to present us before himself without any stain, without any sin, without any *blame*. The charges have been dropped.

Do you get that? The only one with the right to accuse us *doesn't*.

Because of the gospel, we can never face a double jeopardy situation. We can never be tried again on these charges. The record of debt that stood against us, with all of its legal demands, has been canceled; he has nailed it to the cross (2:14).

As in the United States court system, once a verdict is rendered in a case, that case cannot be tried again. If you're brought to trial and found not guilty, the prosecution cannot take another run at you. They can't drum up more evidence for a do-over. They may believe you're guilty. But if you've been declared innocent in a court of law, that's the end of the legal matter.

There's no double jeopardy in American justice. And there's no double jeopardy in the divine justice of the cross. Christ has satisfied the debt "once for all" (Heb. 10:10; 1 Pet. 3:18).

This side of heaven, after our conversion, we absolutely still struggle with sin. But even this disobedience won't condemn us, because the blood of Christ "speaks a better word" than even the blood, sweat, and tears of our obedience (Heb. 12:24 ESV). And when we repent of our sin and put our faith in Jesus, he doesn't simply forgive our sins for all time; our faith is credited to us as righteousness! In other words, it's not just Christ's cross that's considered ours, it's also Christ's perfection. The theologians call this the doctrine of *imputation*. Basically, Christ's perfect obedience to the Father is credited to our spiritual account. Maybe you've heard before that to be *justified* is to be considered "just-as-if-I'd" never sinned. But it also means "just-as-if-I'd" always obeyed.

Our friend Jesus isn't just defending us against the accuser; he is himself not accusing us. He covers us in his irrevocable love, commits eternally to perfect in us what he has begun, and guarantees that when we stand before the great throne of judgment at the end of the age, we have no need to fear a trial. If we've pled the blood of Christ, the blood of Christ will ever be our plea.

Because of these truths, we can live every day, come what may, in confidence and joy. Even in our suffering and hardship, we can rejoice. If we're friends with Jesus, the most important trial we could ever face has been settled. We don't have to prove ourselves to him. We don't have to measure up. We don't have to impress him. Every Christian wakes up with Jesus as a ready and eager friend. And no matter how the day has gone—and you might have really blown it!—every Christian goes to bed at night with Jesus as a ready and eager friend.

As the hymn goes, "What a friend we have in Jesus!"[3]

Our great friend's own brother, the apostle Jude, ends his little treatise on the importance of theological orthodoxy with a similar refrain, writing this doxological tribute:

> Now to him who is able to protect you from stumbling and to make you stand in the presence of his glory, without blemish and with great joy, to the only God our Savior, through Jesus Christ our Lord, be glory, majesty, power, and authority before all time, now and forever. Amen. (Jude 24–25)

The Defense Rests

Isn't it a relief to know that, because of Christ, you no longer face a divine prosecution? And doesn't it change the way you relate to God himself?

Jesus tells a story about two guys who go up to the temple to pray (Luke 18:9–14). One is a religious leader, a Pharisee. The other is a tax collector, a category of people considered especially sinful in Jesus's day. Jesus says, "The Pharisee was standing and praying like this about himself: 'God, I thank you that I'm not like other people—greedy, unrighteous, adulterers, or even like this tax collector. I fast twice a week; I give a tenth of everything I get'" (vv. 11–12). The tax collector, on the other hand, "kept striking his chest and saying, 'God, have mercy on me, a sinner!'" (v. 13).

Jesus says it's the sinful guy who goes home justified.

The Pharisee is recounting all of his alleged successes to the judge, trying to make the case that he's holier than the other guy, all because he thinks the prosecution will be swayed by his own merit. What he doesn't understand is that pleading innocent is the best way to retain his guilt forever. Instead, if he throws himself on the mercy of the court, readily admitting his guilt like the tax collector, he'd see the charges against him dropped.

When we repent of our sin and place our faith in Jesus, we're admitting that we don't have what it takes to earn the salvation he has purchased for each of us. Turning to follow Christ is a waving of the white flag of surrender. It's our way of saying we have no hope except in Christ.

Therefore, when we spend our time in the divine dialogue trying to impress God, we're missing the point. God isn't impressed by us. And there's nothing we can do to earn his favor. He's already freely given it to us in Christ. Our Bible reading isn't earning credit with God. And our prayers don't have to be defensive.

You can rest from trying to make your case. The Lord has already accepted you.

But, you think, *I really messed up today. I let God down. He has to be extremely disappointed in me. And I keep on letting him down. Surely he's going to be done with me any day now.*

Not a chance. The gospel is a binding verdict. You can start new every day, because his mercies are new every day (Lam. 3:22–23). You wake up justified. If you've become friends with Jesus, the case is over. The law against double jeopardy is in effect.

The Lord never asks you to impress him. He never asks you to prove yourself to him. He never asks you to pay him back. And he never asks you to earn his grace. He loves and accepts you; there's no need to put on airs, pad your résumé, or puff yourself up.

How then should we relate to Jesus? If our defense can rest in his presence, what can we safely bring to him? First, we can confess our sins freely. Sin isn't safe with Jesus, but sinners definitely are. He is the sinner's only refuge from condemnation. We don't have to hide anything in his presence. We can't hide anything from him anyway, so it's best not to waste time trying.

We don't have to be afraid of how he'll receive us. The sooner we own up to our rebellious disobedience, the quicker we'll be reminded that he treats us as beloved children. First John 1:9 says, "If we confess our sins, he is faithful and righteous to forgive us our sins and to cleanse us from all unrighteousness." This is why Jesus instructs his friends to pray for forgiveness (Matt. 6:12)—not because it's hard to pry forgiveness out of God but because God is more eager to forgive than we are to repent!

Because Christ is an always-flowing fountain of "grace upon grace" (John 1:16), we don't have to hold anything back. We can bring our whole selves into the light and confess with abandon.

Second, though, because we can rest our defense in his presence, we don't have to wallow in the sins we confess. Jesus commends the tax collector in his story for freely admitting he's a sinner, but we assume this confessor is truly trusting God will have mercy on him. We assume God is going to forgive the man. What we hope *doesn't* happen is that the man keeps beating his chest and crying out in anguish because he thinks his sin is somehow more powerful than God's grace.

It may feel like a kind of humility, but when we plunk ourselves down in defeat and adopt an identity of victimhood in relation to our sin, we're actually exalting ourselves in a very insidious way. It might look like humility, but acting like our sin is unconquerable is an odd kind of pride. God hasn't met his match with any of us. Because his mercy is greater than our sin and his grace more powerful than our flesh, we can drop the self-pity act. That's not any more impressive to him than a recitation of our religious accomplishments.

One of the goals of relating to Christ through the divine dialogue is a profound self-unconsciousness. Self-awareness is good; we wouldn't know what sins to confess or what behaviors to suppress if we weren't at least somewhat self-aware.

But self-consciousness—that slapping on the makeup, putting on the fancy clothes, putting on our best self kind of impression-making—is a fast track to a fake relationship with the idea of Jesus.

The real Jesus wants the real you. So you can stop trying to ward him off with faux humility.

And finally, because we can rest our defense in Christ's presence, we can expect to be set free from our sin. It doesn't enslave us anymore. It doesn't define us anymore. We don't have to be constantly digging through our old case files, revisiting the burdens of our sketchy past.

You can live today in the light of Christ, free from the sin and pain of your past, because Christ himself has decided to effectively lose those files.

The prophet declares, "He will vanquish our iniquities. [He] will cast all our sins into the depths of the sea" (Mic. 7:19). Corrie ten Boom comments on this promise that after God throws our sins into the salty depths, he puts a sign over that spot that reads No Fishing.

In other words, you don't need to keep dredging up what God has buried. You don't need to try to resurrect with your flesh what God has crucified with Christ. And you don't need to go diving around in your regrets and remorse either. If he has cast your sins into the depths of the sea, let them sink. They don't need to rule over you anymore.

In Hebrews 8:12, we're told that God "will never again remember" our sins. The promise is echoed in Hebrews 10:17. In a way, God forgives and "forgets." Now, of course, God is omniscient. He's never truly forgotten anything. But this manner of speaking is important. It's telling us that God's choosing to un-remember our transgressions against him.

This is his strong way of expressing how he is not holding our sins against us. It's almost like we approach him to confess a sin, and on the foundation of Christ's blood and because of our very humble contrition in the moment, he looks at us and says, "What are you talking about?"

You can knock down your walls. You can lower the drawbridge to your heart. In Jesus's presence, you can uncross your arms and legs and you can look him in the eye. He's not waiting for an excuse to let you have it. The trial is over. The cross is definitive. Love has won.

God, in his Word, tells us that he is love (1 John 4:8). And he tells us that love doesn't keep a record of wrongs (1 Cor. 13:5). So rest in this implication of the gospel: God isn't keeping score. Because his Son is victorious, so are you. Because his Son is beloved, so are you. And because his Son is eternally resting from the work of atonement, so are you.

"It is finished" means "case closed."

7

Shooting Straight

(Jesus the Honest Friend)

> Batter my heart, three-person'd God; for you
> As yet but knock, breathe, shine, and seek to mend;
> That I may rise, and stand, o'erthrow me, and bend
> Your force, to break, blow, burn, and make me new.
>
> John Donne, "Holy Sonnet 14"[1]

There's no friend more honest than Jesus. He is always truthful; he is truth *full*, because he is himself the Truth (John 14:6). Therefore, he cannot lie. He's not like us.

Jesus doesn't spin or obfuscate either. He's never trying to put one over on us, working some self-serving angle at our expense. He won't exploit anybody. He's not like us.

When it comes to hard conversations, Jesus won't mince words. He doesn't do passive aggression. He doesn't gossip. He doesn't manipulate. He doesn't berate. He's not like us.

You and I have real trouble with the truth. We like it when it exalts us, but we hate it when it doesn't. As it pertains to offense or criticism, we'll insist the "truth must come out" when it applies to other people, especially people we don't particularly like, but we prefer it to be suppressed or ignored when it applies to us. We'll manage our images, tell white lies, even engage in outright cover-ups if we know the truth is costly.

Jesus knows the truth is often costly. But he's committed to speaking it—and seeing us walk in it—anyway. You will never get anything from Jesus but God's honest truth. He's not like us.

Think of the friend in your circle everyone looks to when it's time to have a hard conversation. We all have one, maybe two. Something needs to be addressed with a mutual friend. Nobody wants to get the job done. We hate conflict. We don't want to take the risk. We feel awkward. But we have that one friend we can trust with the task. He or she doesn't mind difficult conversations and doesn't shrink back at awkwardness. He or she appears qualified, and so gets the job.

When I was pastoring, I sometimes wished I had a fellow elder who could be a bulldog. All those I served with were known for their gentleness, their calmness, their obvious pastoral disposition. The downside to this is that such people often tend toward passivity when it comes to even necessary conflict. They're not always confident leaders in times that call for reproval or rebuke. I mean, *I* didn't want to do those things either! Which is why I daydreamed about adding a pastoral bulldog to the team.

I'm aware that some pastoral teams seem to consist *only* of bulldogs. That's a problem of a different sort. When you have a circle full of folks who don't mind conflict and seem wired for hard conversations, the temptations are great toward a domineering ministry, a quarrelsome spirit, or even an abusive environment.

The key to addressing conflict in a biblical way is neither passivity nor eagerness but a gentle spirit imbued with confidence. This is the way of Jesus. "I am lowly and humble in heart," Christ says (Matt. 11:29). He comes not to crush but to care. If what he says or does hurts, it's only a necessary correction on our way to healing, like a doctor might need to rebreak a bone to set it right. Jesus is love embodied. And love refuses to perpetuate dishonesty or mollycoddle sin but instead "rejoices in the truth" (1 Cor. 13:6).

Jesus is that friend who will tell us the truth, even if it does hurt sometimes. (Okay, a lot of times.) But he isn't a friend who enjoys making us squirm. He's not a guy who likes to see us flinch. Jesus isn't abusive.

This doesn't mean Jesus is never intimidating. He's quite intimidating, in fact, especially when first we get to know him. He is the fearsome God in the flesh. But he's also a genuine friend. I'm reminded of Mrs. Beaver in the Narnia stories describing the lion Aslan as not safe but good.

Still, for those who seek refuge in him, Jesus is the safest person who has ever existed. Not even the devil can get at us in the fortress of Christ. Jesus isn't a tame lion, but he's a good one.

My friend Ray is the embodiment of this paradox of intimidating and comfortable. I've written about Ray in several of my books, and I don't have a problem adding one more, because the man is fascinating. When I first met him, over coffee in Franklin, Tennessee, I was immediately struck by the piercing nature of his gaze. Ray makes eye contact in an overwhelming way. As we chatted about church planting and the gospel in that first meeting, I kept nervously wondering where I was supposed to look. To avert my gaze seemed rude, but looking him in the eye was freaking me out. It felt like he was looking into my soul.

There's just something slightly "off" about Ray—but in a good way! The more I got to know him, the more time I spent with him, the more I could say I became accustomed to the intensity of his gaze, but I couldn't say I ever got used to it.

There are some people who look at you, and you sense there's nothing much behind their eyes. Their gaze is intense because it's cold and piercing in an unsafe way. Ray's uncanny ability isn't like that. It's warm, cheerful, and penetrating in a way I can only credit to the divine. It isn't the kind of intimidation adopted by those hoping to "win." He isn't positioning himself for power.

Ray's intimidating presence is as far from the world's attempts to diminish and demoralize as east is from west. I don't even think he's *trying* to do anything. He's just being himself and wanting me to be me. He's just walking in the truth. But this stands in stark relief against the baseline adulteration of everyday life in a fallen world. Every time I visit with my friend, I walk away feeling simultaneously convicted and empowered. It's a rare combination. Most people you and I interact with trend one way or the other. They make us feel convicted or challenged but without a sense of encouragement or empowerment, which can only result in a feeling of condemnation. Or they seek to inspire or empower but without a right-sizing of our challenges or flaws, which only amounts to flattery, blowing smoke. The best friends have the ability to challenge us without crushing us and inspire us without puffing us up.

I used to jokingly say that the reason Ray is like this is because half of him exists in heaven already. He walks around in a bifurcated space, partially submerged in the spiritual plane. I have decided that this isn't far off the mark. I realized at some point why Ray is the way Ray is: *he actually knows Jesus.*

Ray's indeed the most Jesusy guy I've ever known. And I know he could have gotten that way only by spending lots and lots of time with Jesus. There's a purity to Ray's disposition, an unabashed "what you see is what you get" quality, full of truth and empty of pretense, that makes him an ideal straight shooter. Spending lots of time with Jesus will have that effect.

Friendship Is Knowing

"What were you thinking?"

I was sitting in the backyard of a friend, each of us in lawn chairs, drinking root beer and trying hard to have a conversation. He had been my best friend, and we spent multiple hours a week together, talking about God and literature, sharing our dreams for the future and hopes for our careers. We'd also spent a lot of time cutting up, making fun of each other and laughing. But this day was different. We were fumbling about in our conversation, going in fits and starts. It wasn't fun. We made a few jokes, but they landed flat. The terms of our relationship had changed. How? He'd cheated on his wife and lost his ministry employment because of it.

He was about to move away, and we were getting together for one last hang, but even after spending so much time together for several years, I struggled because I kept getting this nagging feeling that I didn't know him at all.

"What were you thinking?" I asked at some point.

He didn't want to talk about it. I didn't either. But I knew if we were real friends, we had to. It wasn't because I wanted him to feel condemned. I wasn't going to reject him or treat him like a dirty sinner. And I know my hurt was not as great as his wife's. But I was still hurt. I just couldn't quite figure out how to express it.

And then I realized what bothered me most. It wasn't that my friend turned out to be a sinner. I already knew that. What bothered me was that he had been living this secret life for a long time, and I had no idea. It made me wonder if we were really friends at all.

I've had a few friends who blew up their lives with extramarital affairs. Sitting in the wreckage a bit with them after the fact, I've tried to do my best to remind them of the gospel and of the nearness of Jesus. Some of these times have been harder than others. In each circumstance, I wanted to prove myself a true friend, but in every instance I was also dealing with an overwhelming sense of disorientation. Because without exception, I didn't see any of these failings coming. I didn't notice any red flags.

Oh, sure, there are things in retrospect that make a different kind of sense than they did in the moment. For example, the friend I just told you about drew somewhat distant for several months before his personal implosion, but his explanations at the time—of dealing with sickness and trying to finish a demanding work project—seemed plausible to me.

What I'm saying is, I didn't have a reason not to trust him. I didn't have a reason not to trust any of these guys. But each time as I heard the news of their moral failing, my heart was broken not just for their sin and the grief they caused their family but for a friendship that apparently wasn't what it seemed.

To be clear, I'm not saying I'm a victim of any of these guys. It's just that these tragedies have prompted a fair amount of self-evaluation. *Why do I keep getting surprised by this? Am I missing anything? Could I have stopped it by being a better friend? Am I asking the right questions? Am I not getting personal enough? Am I just terrible at discernment?*

Times like these are, for me, a gut check. If we were real friends, I figure, I would've seen it coming. I would've known. *Am I not a good enough friend?* And then I remember there are plenty of things I've hidden from my friends. Small things, big things. Things I fear will ruin the friendship. Things I fear will ruin their image of me.

Sometimes friendships operate in a weird kind of relational stasis, with an unspoken agreement that neither party will get particularly deep. "You don't ask me anything invasive, and I'll return the favor." That way we can make sure the friendship works.

But I don't think that's real friendship.

I know the reasons we hide. We aren't willing to be known even by our friends sometimes because we don't want to lose them. We'd rather have a relationship full of deception than not to have one at all.

When I sit down with Jesus, I know that his knowing me isn't contingent upon my confession. I cannot keep him in the dark. Jesus is never surprised by the truth. And yet . . . he always sits down with me. Our friendship isn't jeopardized by his knowing every terrible thing about me. And I can know that our friendship is real. He sees everything, and at no point does he say, "You know what? You're not who I thought you were. I'm sorry, but this isn't going to work out. I'm done."

Every time I drag my sorry self into the divine dialogue, my secrets in tow, Jesus is glad to see me. He will help me sort through it all. He can do that without feeling overwhelmed or disoriented and without questioning the friendship. He can do that because he saw it all coming.

See, real friendship is knowing. We've seen it all and we keep going. In a way, finally seeing each other as we truly are is when we have the opportunity to be real friends. I'm still pretty close with some of the guys I know who made an absolute wreck of their lives. Others I'm no longer close with, but we still chat from time to time. Some I haven't talked to in years. Sometimes that's their fault. Sometimes it's mine. Mostly it's just how things in life happened to shake out. Knowing the truth doesn't always have the same effect. Sometimes it ends a friendship. But other times it sustains one.

Friendship with Christ is one of the most exciting possibilities in the world, if only because it's a relationship consisting of complete knowledge. Jesus has, in fact, always known us. In Romans 8:29, Paul writes, "For those he foreknew he also predestined to be conformed to the image of his Son, so that he would be the firstborn among many brothers and sisters." The foreknowledge the apostle references here is a relational knowledge. It isn't simply that God sees in advance what we're going to do—though that's certainly true too—but that he knows in advance who we are.

Before there even was a you to know, Jesus knew you.

He really knows each of us. He really sees us. That Samaritan woman Jesus intercepts at Jacob's well in John 4 goes back to her town and tells everybody, "Come, see a man who told me everything I ever did" (v. 29). And those people seek Jesus out, in part, I assume, because the prospect of being known that fully by the Messiah is a prospect too delicious to leave unexplored.

The scene of Jesus's call upon the life of Nathanael is telling in this regard, as well:

> Philip found Nathanael and told him, "We have found the one Moses wrote about in the law (and so did the prophets): Jesus the son of Joseph, from Nazareth."
>
> "Can anything good come out of Nazareth?" Nathanael asked him.
>
> "Come and see," Philip answered.
>
> Then Jesus saw Nathanael coming toward him and said about him, "Here truly is an Israelite in whom there is no deceit."
>
> "How do you know me?" Nathanael asked.
>
> "*Before Philip called you, when you were under the fig tree, I saw you*," Jesus answered.
>
> "Rabbi," Nathanael replied, "You are the Son of God; you are the King of Israel!" (1:45–49, emphasis added)

Jesus remarks first that Nathanael (elsewhere called Bartholomew) is a man of truth ("in whom there is no deceit"). Nathanael, not one to just take a compliment, I guess, asks how in the world Jesus could know that. And Jesus tells him, basically, "I've been watching you forever." He gives him a specific moment, a private moment (under the fig tree), that apparently clarifies for Nathanael the penetrating vision of Jesus.

Remember, there aren't any security cameras or location tracking apps at this time. Jesus is a walking security camera and tracking app. He could see Nathanael when no one else could. So Nathanael in this moment feels intimately seen and totally known.

It's no wonder, then, that he responds with a collection of honorifics for Jesus. He calls him Rabbi, which means "teacher." He calls him the Son of God, which is an ascription of deity. And he calls him the King of Israel, which is a clear attribution of Messiahship. He is piling up the titles for our Lord. Nathanael feels so known by Jesus in this moment that he responds with multiple facets of Jesus's person and vocation. Jesus has identified him for what he truly is, and Nathanael wants to return the favor. It's a way of saying, "I want to know you like you know me!" And it's the beginning of a beautiful friendship.

The ministry of Jesus's twelve disciples is one full of mistakes and duplicity. These guys have the best seminary education in the world—living side by side with God in the flesh for three straight years!—and yet they're incredibly slow learners. If you're a close reader of the four Gospels, you'll notice straightaway how these followers aren't the sharpest knives in the drawer. Is Jesus just bad at picking talent? Is he fooled by their résumés? Their big talk?

Of course not. He knows exactly what he's getting into. He knows exactly who he's calling. He knows James and John will jockey for position. He knows Peter will deny him at the most crucial of moments. He knows Judas is a greedy betrayer. He knows Matthew, being a tax collector, will be a liability to his credibility in most circles.

Jesus knows he is recruiting dirtbags and losers. He knows he is calling sinners. He knows them inside and out. But he calls them anyway. He gets up close and personal with them. And something remarkable happens to them. With the exception of Judas, whose falling away is also foreknown, these men emerge from all their flaws and failings, because of Christ's faithful commitment to them, to be unleashed into the world as agents of change themselves.

Just as Jesus could touch a leper and restore his flesh, or speak over a tomb and see a body come stumbling out, he touches the hearts of these men and utterly remakes them. It is through their mission that he begins to remake the world. He knows them, and he makes sure they know him.

To be a disciple is to be changed. To be known is to change.

You can doubt this change, if you like. You can try quenching the Spirit. But Jesus is no respecter of personal space. He's not a polite kind of friend. Come to him crooked, and he will shoot you straight.

In Genesis 32:24–31, we read of Jacob wrestling with God.

Jacob was left alone, and a man wrestled with him until daybreak. When the man saw that he could not defeat him, he struck Jacob's hip socket as they wrestled and dislocated his hip. Then he said to Jacob, "Let me go, for it is daybreak."

But Jacob said, "I will not let you go unless you bless me."

"What is your name?" the man asked.

"Jacob," he replied.

"Your name will no longer be Jacob," he said. "It will be Israel because you have struggled with God and with men and have prevailed."

Then Jacob asked him, "Please tell me your name."

But he answered, "Why do you ask my name?" And he blessed him there.

Jacob then named the place Peniel, "For I have seen God face to face," he said, "yet my life has been spared." The sun shone on him as he passed by Penuel—limping because of his hip.

The moment is fascinating. The man with whom Jacob gets into this wrestling match is likely a preincarnate appearance of the Son of God. We assume this because Jacob says as much: "I have seen God face to face."

We can learn a lot about God by wrestling with him. I don't advise it, but we all end up doing it from time to time anyway. We know we can't win, not really. But we try. And if we do it in such a way that we're looking for a blessing, we cannot leave the ring unchanged.

The Lord gets so personal with Jacob, having made him and knowing him inside and out, that he changes his name. (This is something God does throughout the Scriptures. It's a symbol not just of his sovereign authority over us but of his fatherly relationship with us.) And Jacob goes away limping.

We can't get close to Jesus and walk away unchanged. To be friends with Jesus, with all the messiness and wrestling it may entail, is to be made new.

Friendship Is Being Known

Jesus sees each of us like he saw Nathanael. He knows who we are when no one is looking. There's no place we can hide from his all-seeing gaze (Ps. 139:1–16).

Remember back in chapter 1, when I was ranting about the growing fundamentalism of tribes on both the right and the left? I mentioned the horseshoe theory, the idea that the further to the extremes one goes in either direction, the closer one gets to the extreme of the other side. I find this supposition very satisfying. It explains a lot about what I experience in a lot of social circles, especially online. I find myself in the middle of these extremes quite often. I'm in the center of that horseshoe, feeling the pull from both sides, all the while crying out for everybody to see what I see.

Now, imagine in one of my visits with Jesus, I explain to him how awful this whole situation is. I complain about the jerks on the right and the jerks on the left. I appeal to his justice. Can't he sort it all out? Wouldn't it be wonderful if those folks would wake up, realize they're acting like idiots, and repent? I think so.

I suggest to Jesus that he gather these tribes around a table and give a lecture. Set everybody straight. And I'm pleased to hear that he will oblige. The day comes, and representatives of both tribes are seated. Left-wing political nutjobs and right-wing political wackos. Heretical religious lefties and pharisaical religious fundies. Jesus sits at the end of the table, naturally, and I stand over his shoulder, smiling. *Finally*, I think.

Then Jesus turns to face me and says, "Have a seat."

"Me?" I say. "Oh. Okay."

I squeeze in next to him.

Then Jesus gives a good talking-to, like I hoped he would. Like I asked him to. But I didn't realize he was going to be talking *to me*.

"Jared," he says, "you see so clearly the sins of those seated at this table. You're obviously very concerned about them.

About their sins, I mean. But there's one thing you haven't seen as clearly."

I'm a little dumbfounded. It's not going like I thought it would.

"It's yourself," Jesus continues. "You imagine yourself at the center of these extremes as if there's no extremism in your own heart. You sit in judgment against those who don't think or act like you do, and you're satisfied in your not sinning like they do. You're like the man who goes into the temple, thanking my Father that you aren't like 'them.'"

"Well, I, uh . . . ," I sputter.

But I'm caught. I've been found out. It's useless to defend myself. Like the disciples in Luke 9:54–55, I wanted fire called down on my enemies, and Jesus has turned to rebuke me.

The truth is, Jesus knows I'm trying to be above it all. My "third way" may be the right position to take, but he knows I'm proud of it. He knows I think of myself as being above it all, of occupying some hallowed place of holy neutrality. He sees all my attempts to deflect and judge. He knows my biggest problem is me.

This is something that happens to me over and over again in my relationship with Jesus. I bring to him, in so many words, my complaints and criticisms about others, my insistence that life would be so much easier if all of "those people" would just act right, and he reminds me that "those people" have their own relationships with him to work out. When he and I are alone, we can only deal with me.

When I was doing a lot of pastoral counseling, I used to remind my counselees of this truth as well. Most people come in with relationship troubles or other complaints related to their treatment at the hands of others, and I'd typically spot them one session to get out all the stuff about what others should do. This wasn't me saying they were wrong about any of it! And very often, I could suggest some practical ways to address others to seek resolution, reconciliation, or even justice. But I'd remind them of the reality that all of the other people with problems were not in the room. And we can't control other people anyway. "We can only control ourselves," I'd say. "So let's talk about what *we* can do."

Jesus has been great at giving me a taste of my own medicine.

I try asking about this person or that person, and he says, "What is that to you? As for you, follow me" (John 21:22). He knows that I'm self-centered, self-justifying, and self-exalting. And he wants me to know it too.

As it turns out, it's a good thing to know ourselves. Knowing ourselves helps us see Christ as more glorious. If I think I'm hot stuff, I won't be nearly as impressed by his glory. In fact, a part of me will act as if I kind of deserve what he did for me. But if I know myself, I know my need and my sin, and I will see him better—see him for who he truly is.

Jesus is a straight shooter for my good. He's not trying to crush my spirit but my pride. He tells me the truth about myself so that I will know myself better and thus know him better too. "The wounds of a friend are trustworthy," Proverbs 27:6 tells us.

In fact, Jesus wouldn't be my friend if he wasn't trustworthily wounding me like this. He wouldn't be my friend if he was just suffering my selfishness gladly.

What about you? What truth about yourself is Jesus wanting you to face? Whatever it is, you can take it. Coming from him means its source is a place of deep love and grace. If it came from anybody else, you could suspect malice in it. But from Christ, the painful truth is faithful.

That thing you don't want to talk about or even think about, that thing you try to hide, that thing everybody else wants you to face but you've avoided and turned around and blamed them for—you can face it head-on. Because your faithful friend is with you. And real friendship with him means being known. It means surrendering to him access to the deepest and most broken parts of yourself.

The truth may sting, but only like the shot of an antidote you need for the poison that's already killing you. Take the risk of being known. It's far less risky than the alternative. And it's the only means of experiencing newness. Jesus plans to set you free.

The Truth Will Set Us Free

When I was living a life of hidden sin, Jesus saw me. I thought I was keeping everything nice and secret, but he knew every hidden thing (Dan. 2:22). Then it all came out. I couldn't keep up the religious façade. It destroyed me. Everyone who mattered in my life could see the deepest, grossest parts of me. Naturally, they withdrew. I had betrayed them. I wasn't who they thought I was. I wasn't who I said I was.

But my Savior didn't recoil. He came closer.

It was in my lowest, most broken, most desperate devastation that Christ came near in the sweetest grace and care. My sin didn't surprise him. My blowing up my life did not startle him.

He saw it all coming, and in a way, I was on a collision course with a life-changing awakening to the gospel, sovereignly directed by his own will. The truth caught up with me, but so did the grace of God. And when I was most exposed, he was the most tender. "He will not break a bruised reed," Isaiah 42:3 says, "and he will not put out a smoldering wick."

I have felt that.

Having learned, slowly and painfully, that Christ can be trusted with the real me, day by day I'm more inclined to present my real self to him. I don't make as many invitations for others to join us at that table for a talking-to anymore! I know it's just for Jesus and me. I sit across from him and invite him into the deepest parts of my life, the parts he most wants to deal with.

I know he has all the wisdom needed for my biggest confusion. He has all the strength needed for my biggest weakness. And he has all the grace needed for my biggest sin. You can know this too. Because he knows you. He sees you. While you pray, Jesus's eyes are open.

"Therefore," Hebrews 4:16 encourages us, "let us approach the throne of grace with boldness, so that we may receive mercy and find grace to help us in time of need." For all of our lack, our friend Jesus has a steady supply. He knows what we need when we need it. He knows what we should hear when we need to hear it. He even knows when we're *not* ready.

In John 16:12, Jesus looks at his disciples in love and says, "I still have many things to tell you, but you can't bear them now." I don't know why, but this verse sends a thrill to my heart. First of all, it sounds so pastoral. Jesus is such a Good Shepherd; he knows when to call us to carry a load and when not to. He knows our capacity as creatures. He ministers to us well in our frailty. Second, I just love that Jesus is promising that even after all the great stuff he's done for us, shown us, and promised us, there's still more to come!

"You're not ready for this yet," he's saying. "But just wait. I've got more for you."

There is no friend so *helpfully* honest as Jesus. He won't load us down with truth. It's designed and positioned for our good. His burden, remember, is easy. His yoke is light. He doesn't call us servants but friends. He has come to give us rest. He has come to give us nothing short of resurrection! Through thick and thin, we can rely on Jesus the straight shooter to steer us right—and to steer us *right into glory*.

Because we can count on Jesus to always tell us the truth, then, we can trust him when he calls us his friend. We don't have to wonder. You can still wonder, if you want. And you probably will at times. But you don't have to. You've never had a friend you need to worry about less than Jesus. You don't need to worry about him at all.

Yes, the truth will hurt sometimes. If Jesus didn't love us, he'd just smother us in lies. Because he loves us, though, sometimes he steers things to our disappointment, even our discipline (Prov. 3:12; Heb. 12:16).

But the truth also heals. It thrills. The truth changes us, makes us new, and lifts us up into heretofore unimaginable glory. Because the truth is

he loves you.

he died for you.

he rose for you.

he will defend you.

he will stay by you.

And he'll raise you up on the last day, glorified as all get-out.

That's the kind of truth-telling friend we have. The kind whose truth sets us free from sin and death. He's the kind of friend who liberates us from the old way of being ourselves so we can be free, as Romans 6:4 says, to "walk in newness of life."

8

And the Kitchen Sink

(*Jesus the Generous Friend*)

Coming sinner, whatever promise you find in the Word of Christ, strain it as much as you can, so long as you do not corrupt it, and his blood and merits will answer all.

John Bunyan, *Come and Welcome to Jesus Christ*[1]

There is no friend so generous as Jesus. He's the friend who wants more for you than you want for yourself. He's the friend who, when he comes over for dinner or game night, always brings flowers or a bottle of wine. He's the one who, when he's hosting you, is always going to send you home with that book you admired on his shelf or that extra tool he doesn't have any use for or at least a bag full of delicious leftovers. Jesus is the friend who is constantly giving.

He's like this because there's nothing he needs. Jesus is perfectly content in his own being. He has no deficiencies, no diminishment. I suppose this is why he instructs his followers to give even their jackets to anyone who just asked for a shirt (Matt. 5:40). "Give to the one who asks you," Jesus says, "and don't turn away from the one who wants to borrow from you" (v. 42).

Astonishingly, Jesus even says that if we ask from him, we will receive (Mark 11:24). Of course, we may not receive exactly what we expected, but we'll always receive what we need. He won't leave us hanging. Remember, he told the woman at the well that he could give her living water that would make it so she'd never be thirsty again (John 4:10). That's a steady supply, never-ending. Ask once, and you're set up to be satisfied in perpetuity.

Jesus doesn't even always wait for us to ask. He's so generous, he just constantly gives out of his own storehouse, on his own initiative. Paul says in Ephesians 3:20 that Christ goes "above and beyond" what we even think to ask for, beyond what we can even imagine. When we don't know how to ask, Christ's Spirit is making requests on our behalf (Rom. 8:26).

The friend who knows what you need before you even realize it—that's a great friend. That's a friend who knows you well, who is tuned in to your life with all of its problems and possibilities. Sometimes when I bring my wife something so simple as a cup of coffee made just the way she likes it— more cream than coffee—she will say, "How did you know I needed that?" The answer to that question is rather long, but the short version is I know her. I not only know how she likes her coffee but that she for some reason thinks coffee made by someone else always tastes better than coffee she makes herself, even if it's made the same way. I know she likes a cup after she's gotten out of bed and is preparing for her morning Bible study. I know she likes one in the afternoon when she's ready to take a break from all her work and sit down for a moment. I know she likes one in the evenings, when she feels a little bit chilly, even in our warm living room in the middle of summer. I know these things the same way she knows what I need when I most need it, often before I even know it.

Jesus is a friend like that. In his epistle, James, Jesus's own brother, says God "gives to all generously and ungrudgingly" (1:5). He holds nothing back. For any of us to be generous like this would require holding things loosely. It'd mean seeing people as more important than property, souls as superior to stuff. And it would require our holding ourselves loosely as well—not idolizing comfort and convenience, not centering our lives on accumulating things or wealth.

For Jesus to be generous like this requires him to, in a sense, hold *himself* loosely. Because the ultimate gift Christ gives us is the perpetual gift of himself. According to Paul, this is the attitude Jesus had:

> Existing in the form of God,
> [he] did not consider equality with God
> as something to be exploited.
> Instead he emptied himself. (Phil. 2:6–7)

Some translations will say that Jesus didn't regard his equality with God as something to be "grasped." In other words, while he never ceased to be God, he held that nature loosely in order to grab hold of us. He didn't exploit his divine privileges and glory to avoid showing the greatest generosity one could show (John 15:13). The Son of God didn't wish us well from heaven or send us good vibes. He got close, put skin on, and gave us his whole life.

All of him for all of us. That's what he gives.

Yes, the whole of Christ's life is a mediation for sinners in desperate need of grace. What I mean is, the mediating work of Christ our substitute isn't wholly contained in his crucifixion and resurrection but begins before creation and extends from his ascension through his ever-present intercession and advocacy for us into the eternality of the future. And this means that from the incarnation of the Son of God all through his earthly ministry, Christ is our mediator. The whole of Christ's life is a mediation for sinners.

His sinless life isn't merely our great example. It is—he is—our great *righteousness*. And perhaps in no place in the four Gospels is this "whole life mediation" more clearly articulated than in Christ's high priestly prayer in John 17. Jesus prays. And in his prayer we receive not just a lot of doctrine but a lot of grace.

What He Gives

The apostle's placement of the high priestly prayer in the chronology of the Passion Week is interesting. There's some dispute about whether John 17 is the full transcript of Christ's Gethsemane prayer or whether it's a pre-Gethsemane prayer, a closing prayer for the so-called farewell discourse that begins in John 14. I honestly don't think it much matters, but while I used to think this prayer was the full recording of Jesus's prayer in the garden, I'm more recently inclined to think this is the climactic moment of his farewell discourse.

In fact, this prayer of Jesus is a culminating moment of his entire earthly ministry of mediation. Indeed, every day of his life he has been interceding in word and deed for the elect, and in this prayer we find a summation of his intercessory work. The prayer is a treasure chest. We open it up to find all the precious jewels of grace John has been highlighting throughout his Gospel in one glorious trove.

Throughout his evangelistic text, John has been presenting a historically accurate accounting of Jesus, but clearly his emphases and his organization are distinct from the other Gospels. It's why Matthew, Mark, and Luke are called the synoptic Gospels—"synoptic" because they look alike. John's Gospel stands apart and is structured more thematically, more explicitly theologically—beginning not with a birth narrative but a cosmic preface echoing Genesis 1 and then subsequently organized around seven signs and their implications. Over and over again, John isn't simply interested in helping us to see Jesus but to *behold* him.

After the apostle John lays out the truth of Christ as the glorious light of the world shining into the darkness, John the Baptist cries out, "Behold, the Lamb of God, who takes away the sin of the world!" (1:29 ESV). Jesus's prayer in John 17 is a beautiful theological bookend to that cosmic opening, an echo of the glory and its impact on sinners in need of grace.

What John is doing with his Gospel he tells us in 20:31. "These are written so that you may believe that Jesus is the Christ, the Son of God, and that by believing you may have life in his name" (ESV). John's Gospel is about the saving revelation of the glory of God in his Son Jesus Christ—his Gospel, in other words, is about *the* gospel.

And this is what Jesus's prayer in John 17 is ultimately about as well. So I want to offer a thirty-thousand-foot view, so to speak, highlighting some important facets of Christ's saving work on behalf of his friends, and as we go, we'll see some of these gleaming jewels Jesus generously gives us. Consider verses 1–8:

> When Jesus had spoken these words, he lifted up his eyes to heaven, and said, "Father, the hour has come; glorify your Son that the Son may glorify you, since you have given him authority over all flesh, to give eternal life to all whom you have given him. And this is eternal life, that they know you, the only true God, and Jesus Christ whom you have sent. I glorified you on earth, having accomplished the work that you gave me to do. And now, Father, glorify me in your own presence with the glory that I had with you before the world existed.
>
> "I have manifested your name to the people whom you gave me out of the world. Yours they were, and you gave them to me, and they have kept your word. Now they know that everything that you have given me is from you. For I have given them the words that you gave me, and they have received them and have come to know in truth that I came from you; and they have believed that you sent me." (ESV)

These words, along with Jesus's later references to being "in the Father" and the Father "being in him" are Christ's self-attesting testimonies to his own deity, his own "God-ness." The shared glory and mission are tightly connected; this isn't simply Jesus saying he's of the same mind as the

Father. He's saying he's of the same "stuff." As in John 10:30, where he says, "I and the Father are one," he doesn't just mean they're in agreement. This is a highlight for John in his repetition of Christ's "I AM" statements throughout his Gospel.

Jesus is fully God. John proclaims in his prologue that the Word wasn't just with God but the Word was God (1:1). And this Word who was God *is* God, for Jesus is the same yesterday, today, and forever. Jesus echoes that when he says, "Father, glorify me in your own presence with the glory that I had with you before the world existed" (17:5 ESV).

In fact, this is how we ought to understand the concept of the Son being the Son. In his incarnation he's submissive to the Father, but in his eternal Sonship he isn't submissive to the Father but equal to the Father, of the same essence as the Father.

That's what's meant by the designation of the Second Person of the Trinity as the "Son." Sonship here doesn't mean he's less than the Father. It means he is *of the same* as the Father. And we have indications of this in John 17.

verse 1 = glorify your Son
verse 5 = preexistent glory
verse 10 = everything you have is mine
verse 11 = your name that you've given me
verse 21 = you, Father, are in me, and I am in you
verse 22 = we are one

All of this is Christ expressing the reality of his own deity (his God-ness), and of his own parity with the Father.

Because Jesus Christ is God, he's an able Savior. He's able to give us a reliable foundation, a secure salvation, and omnipotent help in our time of need. Because no other human is God, no other human can be a friend like Jesus. What no other friend can do, he can. What no other friend could do, he did.

In John 17:4, he says that he has accomplished the work the Father gave him to do. This is but a preface to his cry from the cross, "It is finished" (19:30).

But it's not just that Christ is *able* to save. He has *actually exercised* his ability to save us. In other words, to say that God is able to save isn't exactly the good news, because God is able to do many things that he nevertheless chooses not to do. Whenever he says no to one of our prayers, for instance, we shouldn't construe that to mean he's saying "I can't." (Unless we're asking him to sin or otherwise act against his nature.)

I'm drawing here from John 17:9–19, where Jesus turns from praying for himself to praying for his followers. Christ interceding on sinners' behalf is good news, and here it rises to the surface of his prayer in wonderful relief:

> I am praying for them. I am not praying for the world but for those whom you have given me, for they are yours. All mine are yours, and yours are mine, and I am glorified in them. And I am no longer in the world, but they are in the world, and I am coming to you. Holy Father, keep them in your name, which you have given me, that they may be one, even as we are one. While I was with them, I kept them in your name, which you have given me. I have guarded them, and not one of them has been lost except the son of destruction,

that the Scripture might be fulfilled. But now I am coming to you, and these things I speak in the world, that they may have my joy fulfilled in themselves. I have given them your word, and the world has hated them because they are not of the world, just as I am not of the world. I do not ask that you take them out of the world, but that you keep them from the evil one. They are not of the world, just as I am not of the world. Sanctify them in the truth; your word is truth. As you sent me into the world, so I have sent them into the world. And for their sake I consecrate myself, that they also may be sanctified in truth. (ESV)

Jesus isn't miserly with his friends. He's not stingy or cheap. He gives the best he's got.

He gives us the only kind of life he has within himself: *eternal life*. That's the primary facet of eternal life on display in this passage—the eternality of it—the forever protection Christians have in Christ himself.

verse 10 = those the Father has given to the Son belong to the Father, as all that belongs to the Father also belongs to the Son, meaning we belong to God

verse 11 = the Father is keeping us in his name

verse 12 = he is guarding us, and not one of us will be lost

verse 15 = he will keep us from the evil one

verses 16–17 = he sanctifies us in truth (or sets us apart)

All of these referents point us to the safety we have in Jesus, the everlasting life we have in him. Into his saving work on our behalf, he's thrown everything and the kitchen sink.

Even the loss of the "son of destruction," a reference to Judas Iscariot, isn't an indication of Christ's failure, since he notes that Judas's destruction is according to the divine plan ("that the Scripture might be fulfilled"). In other words, Judas doesn't slip through the cracks. Jesus isn't a pretty good Savior, about to finish the journey eleven for twelve. No, he keeps all who are given to him. None of them are lost. *Nobody slips through the cracks.* If you are saved, you are unconquerably saved. If you're saved, you are eternally saved.

What he gives us first of all is all of his own height and breadth and length and depth. His gift of eternal life comes through his very self.

What He Receives

There then follows in John 17 a pleasant succession of graces named by Christ, as if he's running his hand through his treasure chest and lifting out a variety of jewels to show us the various riches found in his salvation. I'm reminded of John 1:16: "Indeed, we have all received grace upon grace from his fullness."

In Jesus, it's just one grace after another, grace after grace after grace after grace. Christ is an endless fountain of grace—just one drop would be enough to save but still there's an ever-flowing source of life and joy.

I'm drawing now from John 17:20–26, where we see grace upon grace recounted in Christ's final words in his prayer:

I pray not only for these, but also for those who believe in me through their word. May they all be one, as you, Father, are in me and I am in you. May they also be in us, so that the world may believe you sent me. I have given them the glory you have given me, so that they may be one as we are one. I am in them and you are in me, so that they may be made completely one, that the world may know you have sent me and have loved them as you have loved me.

Father, I want those you have given me to be with me where I am, so that they will see my glory, which you have given me because you loved me before the world's foundation. Righteous Father, the world has not known you. However, I have known you, and they have known that you sent me. I made your name known to them and will continue to make it known, so that the love you have loved me with may be in them and I may be in them.

The focus of the intercession turns in verse 20 from his immediate followers to *all* followers for all time. He's making requests for his first-century friends, yes, but also for *us*. For you and me.

And he is here asking for things for us. Gifts!

What are the graces upon graces we see here?

verses 21–23 = the gifts of unity in the church and a compelling witness to the world

verse 24 = the gift of heaven, that we'll be where he is

verse 26 = the gift of the knowledge of God's love

And once you add in the whole prayer, there are even more precious gems like having Christ's joy in ourselves (v. 13) and having Christ's peace. There is no friend so generous as Jesus. As Paul writes in Romans 8:32, "He did not even spare his own Son but gave him up for us all. How will he not also with him grant us everything?" It's just grace upon grace!

But remember those disciples he's praying for. The ones who nap while Jesus intercedes. What has he received from these men? What have they given him? A kind of threadbare loyalty? A self-interested allegiance? Compared to all he's given them, all they've given him is a headache. But he keeps giving; he keeps pouring out. It's almost as if he's *rewarding* their weakness and ineptitude. And in a way, he is—provided they submit those things to him.

Look, even the best works we can muster up for our Lord are puny compared to his glory. It's astonishing to me that he treasures them and turns them into glory for us stored up in the age to come.

This is like when your little son or daughter is out playing in the yard. Wanting to do something special for you, they snatch up a bunch of dandelions or some other weeds and bring them in, beaming as they present them to you. In their mind, they're giving you flowers.

And what do you say? "You idiot, those are weeds."

No, of course you don't say that. You say, "Why, thank you!" A vase or jar is retrieved from the cabinet and filled with fresh water. The "flowers" are placed inside, and the whole thing is displayed on the kitchen counter or the mantel.

Or just think of the copious works of art your children produce with their crayons and finger paints. An endless supply of indiscernible shapes and scribbles. They bring their latest masterpiece to you, and you say, "What a wonderful drawing of a dog!" Your child sheepishly clarifies that it's supposed to be an army truck.

What you don't do is say, "Well, we're not exactly Rembrandt, are we?" No! You thank them for that picture and praise it and tack it to the refrigerator with magnets, because that's where the precious art is displayed in your home.

This is how our friend Jesus receives our stupid efforts at obedience. We bring the weeds of our works and the mess of our efforts to him, and with the warmest gaze, not even pretending, he says, "Oh, how precious!" He is a gracious Savior. Compared to what he's given us, he receives so little. But he gladly accepts it all. He receives everything from us with nothing but love.

Even our sin.

So we ought to be greatly stirred by John 17:20, in which Jesus turns to pray for you and me: "I pray not only for these, but also for those who believe in me through their word." Jesus is here praying for all those who *will* believe, the future believers. That's us.

And I want to believe that, in the space-time economy of the God-Man in this moment, every name and face of every Christian who will ever live is flashing through his mind. I don't know how much time is passing—as long as it takes to read these words, I suppose—but because he and the Father are one, all the attributes of his deity are at his disposal, and in his omniscience, he's able to bring to mind you and me.

Praying for you, he's receiving *you* into *his* heart.

Jesus isn't a potential Savior, he's an able and unconquerable Savior. And he's not a theoretically gracious Savior, he's an *actually gracious* Savior.

You know, whether Jesus prays this prayer in the garden of Gethsemane or in some darkened room doesn't much matter to me. I'm just struck by Christ's bottomless heart for his friends. They are so out of step, so sinful. And the sinless Savior is still interceding for them! If that prayer does take place in the garden, I picture my friend Jesus slumped over in spiritual anguish, practically feeling the splinters of the cross on his back, its shadow looming over him, sweating blood, and his closest buddies *sleeping*.

It's his time of greatest need, and they're napping while he agonizes. And he never says, "That's it. I've had it." No, resolutely, for the joy set before him, he receives the pain and the shame of the cross (Heb. 12:2). He carries it all—*and us*—the whole way through. He's mediating for his disciples while they're too stupid to understand. He's dying for them while most of them are too weak to watch.

He must really love them!

And do you know, he's praying for you while you're sleeping too? At your lowest, worst, most rejectable, he's giving himself to you and for you. Whatever you dish out, he can take. Even while you were a sinner, Christ went to the cross for you (Rom. 5:8). He must really love you.

And if he receives all of our sin, why would he not also receive all of our cares? We can cast those on him too (1 Pet. 5:7).

When all is said and done, what does he receive?

He receives *us*.

What He Is

Jesus means for us to be like him. He's so invested in this task that ultimately he gives his very self to us (Eph. 5:2), laying down his life in our place, uniting us to himself, and dwelling in our hearts by faith. The Giver is himself the gift. And there's no gift he can give us that can exceed the preciousness and worth of his very self.

He is gentle and lowly. He's all-glorious and all-satisfying. He's gracious and merciful. He's loving and kind. Indeed, he's the embodiment of all things true and good. Jesus Christ is "the power of God and the wisdom of God" (1 Cor. 1:24). He is all of these things *for* us and *in* us.

As our Savior's earthly ministry draws to a close, he gathers his closest friends together for a final meal. It's a moment fraught with the tension of what lies ahead, though the disciples still seem somewhat clueless about it. Even so, he wants them to know that what he's sharing with them isn't a meal but his very life. His ministry has always been to give them himself.

> When the hour came, he reclined at the table, and the apostles with him. Then he said to them, "I have fervently desired to eat this Passover with you before I suffer. For I tell you, I will not eat it again until it is fulfilled in the kingdom of God." Then he took a cup, and after giving thanks, he said, "Take this and share it among yourselves. For I tell you, from now on I will not drink of the fruit of the vine until the kingdom of God comes."
>
> And he took bread, gave thanks, broke it, gave it to them, and said, "This is my body, which is given for you. Do this in remembrance of me."
>
> In the same way he also took the cup after supper and said, "This cup is the new covenant in my blood, which is poured out for you." (Luke 22:14–20)

The intimacy of the scene can hardly be overstated. As history is barreling toward the cross, Jesus slows down to recline at the table of fellowship with his friends and commits to them his own flesh and blood.

He has committed his flesh and blood to us too. His body is given for us. And with it comes the eternal goodness only he has within himself. For Christ is all that God is. To have him is to have God. "The one who has seen me," he says, "has seen the Father" (John 14:9). The fullness of deity dwells in Jesus bodily, and this body he gives to us as a perfect gift.

This gift is one of purity and perfection, of authority and dominion, of love and faithfulness. All that we truly need and innately desire is bound up in the gift of Christ.

There is no friend like this! No friends give themselves so freely and without pretense. You and I may do a lot for our friends. We may even give to our friends sacrificially and with joy, genuinely desiring their good and their improvement. But none of us, with even maximum exertion, can give like Jesus gave.

Peter is one of those friends at the table. He thinks he knows what comes next, but he is very wrong. And it's not for lack of being warned. Jesus has told his disciples all along his plans to go to the cross. Matthew 16:22 even records Peter rebuking him for saying it! In a matter of hours after this meal, even after Jesus has told him he would do it, Peter denies his Lord. Three times. But Jesus dies for Peter. He gives his life for him. And as he does for all of us stupid sinners, he gives his life *to* him.

At the Last Supper, Jesus commits to Peter to hold nothing back from him. "This is my body. This is my blood. They are given for you." Peter doesn't realize it then, but later he realizes the gravity of what has taken place. He sees that Jesus isn't simply initiating an ordinance for the church but promising to be each Christian's very sustenance. He comes to see that the Christian life is in its very essence a subsisting on Christ. For Christ himself to become our very life means spiritually and perpetually feeding on him. And by his Spirit, Jesus spiritually and perpetually feeds himself to us.

Perhaps Peter is remembering this very supper when he later declares that Christians are "partakers of the divine nature" (2 Pet. 1:4 ESV). This is a staggering claim. It's a staggering reality. Christ so gives himself to us that we share in all that he is. His nature is portioned to us as spiritual food.

What I mean is, Jesus doesn't simply give us virtues and graces. He is in himself virtue and grace, and he brings us to the place of being "in him" so that we get to partake of him. Peter, writing to Christians in exile and under persecution, reminds believers everywhere that though their circumstances may be full of hardship and uncertainty, they can take hope and find joy in knowing their spirits are full of Jesus.

Every now and again, we may get a pale reflection of this truth in our own earthly fellowship. Have you ever spent a long and leisurely time at a friend's house over a good meal? Sitting around a table, relaxed and carefree, we take our time eating, not simply because the food is delicious but because the spirit of togetherness is delicious too. We reminisce and we laugh. We feel well served and well known. Someone shares a personal story, something that's revelatory, perhaps confessional. Maybe it's us. And the response isn't judgment or even lukewarm toleration. It's understanding, consolation, empathy. The bond of friendship is so strengthened, we may feel closer to them than we do to our own family members.

In moments like these, something more than our stomachs are getting full. When we leave at the end of the evening, our hearts are bursting because we have shared *of each other*.

To be friends with Jesus is like that but more so. We can know that every day he will always be glad to meet with us, to receive us warmly, to hear our deepest fears and our sorrows, our gladdest joys and our basest sins. He will sit with us as long as we're willing to be there with him. And when we push back from the table, ready to go about our day or turn in for the night, we take with us the lingering sense of his fullness, his fondness, his friendship.

To be a partaker of the divine nature is to be brought into the heart of God. C. S. Lewis says that when we draw near to God in prayer, "the whole threefold life of the three-personal Being is actually going on."[2] When we draw near to him to partake of him, his life will swallow us up.

Christ is eager for us to have this experience. He is eager for us to know him this way.

So long as we have breath, this welcome for sinners is always open. And for any of us who will walk through the door of Christ, this door will always be open for us. He's eternally an enthusiastic host. What he is, he will always be. And he will always be for us.

Closeness to Jesus makes us more like Jesus, more like what we someday *will* be. We begin to reflect his gentleness, his peace, his patience, his love, his *everything*, the more we uninterruptedly fellowship with him. The apostle Paul says in 2 Corinthians 3:18 that it's by seeing Christ that we become more Christlike. The closer we walk with him, the more our stride begins to resemble his. We stumble and fumble our way along the journey of faith, but, by God, we are getting somewhere!

He means for us to see him and, by seeing him, to resemble him. And even though our most veteran efforts in the divine dialogue remain but feeble and frail, though we see Jesus only indirectly, one day we will see his face for the first time but as a familiar friend (1 Cor. 13:12). Or, as John puts it, "Dear friends, we are God's children now, and what we will be has not yet been revealed. We know that when he appears, we will be like him because we will see him as he is" (1 John 3:2).

I'm sure that seeing him "as he is" will take our breath away. But it will also be like breathing for the first time. Because no one is more alive than Jesus. And any who give themselves to friendship with Jesus will finally be fully alive.

9

I Just Didn't Want You to Be Alone

(Jesus the Available Friend)

Thine own dear presence to cheer and to guide.

Thomas O. Chisholm,
"Great Is Thy Faithfulness"[1]

There is no friend as perfectly present as Jesus. There is no friend so perfectly *pleasant* as Jesus. He is more than content just to be with you. He won't rush you if you don't need rushing. He won't push you if you don't need pushing. Jesus has all the time in the world. His unhurried presence is perfectly suited for those times we don't know what to do or what to say or where to go or even how to think. Times like these occur more frequently than we realize.

When we're stupidly plowing ahead, steamrolling through life on an appetite-driven autopilot, he waits. He's there when we eventually crash. When we don't have the energy to move forward at all, when the autopilot is busted, our legs don't work, and we feel mired in the quicksand of self-despair or self-pity, he'll be there. He'll take our hand in his and gently but strongly hold us. Sometimes we feel Jesus's presence best when we're at the end of our rope, but he's always been with us. Our lack of feeling isn't his lack of presence.

There's that little story about the man who falls into a deep pit in the woods. Frantic, he tries scrambling up the sides, but he cannot get a handhold or foothold. The loose soil crumbles at his touch. He looks for a root or a rock lodged in the walls of the enclosure but can find none. He begins to shout, calling for help. He yells until his throat is hoarse and his lungs are heaving from exhaustion. Night begins to fall. He is scared. The reality is setting in. He's losing hope he'll ever get out.

The story goes that eventually the man sits down onto the dirty ground and begins to cry. He wonders if he will die down in that pit.

And then overhead, just outside the lip of the deep hole, he hears the dragging of feet. A rescuer! He pictures a ladder being lowered, a rope thrown down to his lonely position. Instead, he sees a body lumber over the side, hands holding on to the edge, and the man's hope turns to confusion as the figure drops straight down into the pit and into a heap alongside him.

When the stranger gathers himself, stands up, and brushes the dust off his pants, he sees it is not a stranger at all, but his friend. "What in the world are you doing?" he says to his would-be rescuer. "Now we're both stuck down here! What were you thinking?"

His friend looks at him, his own confusion evident. He says, "I just didn't want you to be alone."

The moral of the story is, I think, something about the dumbness of a friend who will join you in your predicament without offering a hand out of it. But it has the opposite effect on me. I think of the friends who have drawn near to me in my lowest moments. I can count them on one hand, mainly because I don't often share my lowest moments with most of my friends. I'm too busy pretending I'm living a happy-go-lucky life to let them know I'm in a pit. But sometimes my closest companions know. And they also know shallow pick-me-ups and superficial moralizing won't get me out of the depths anyway. Instead, they just clamber in beside me.

I think of the friends of Job, who, before they start saying some absolutely unhelpful things to their horrifically afflicted friend, just sit with him. Job loses his children, his home, his possessions, his livelihood, and his health. He's sitting in a heap of ashes, scraping boils off his skin with shards of pottery, when his friends show up.

Now when Job's three friends—Eliphaz the Temanite, Bildad the Shuhite, and Zophar the Naamathite—heard about all this adversity that had happened to him, each of them came from his home. They met together to go and sympathize with him and comfort him. When they looked from a distance, they could barely recognize him. They wept aloud, and each man tore his robe and threw dust into the air and on his head. Then they sat on the ground with him seven days and nights, but no one spoke a word to him because they saw that his suffering was very intense. (Job 2:11–13)

In the Jewish tradition, this practice is called "sitting shiva." It's a time of silent solidarity, where mourners gather with one grieving and simply enter into the grief. Sometimes the greatest comfort comes, at least initially, not with words of encouragement but with simply drawing near and seeking to feel the pain, as much as possible, of the one who is hurting.

Jesus is a friend who sits shiva. He'll carry your burdens by getting under them alongside you. Jesus has never been above sitting in the dirt with you.

Certainly, Jesus is more than capable of rescuing anybody out of any hole they find themselves in. But we know from experience he doesn't always do that, at least not right away. Sometimes he wants us to be in the hole for a while, perhaps to grow our faith, regain our strength, or restore some perspective. But however long he wants us there, we know he'll be with us.

I served under a leader once whom I trusted really loved me. He confided in me, encouraged me, and commended me to others. It just so happened that during this ministry assignment, I was in a very low place. The leader above him, our superior, was a borderline spiritual abuser. I felt particularly hurt by that man. And there were other things going on in my life that were causing deep feelings of pain and doubt. So I'd tell my immediate supervisor about them. He was the kind of guy who liked fixing things. He would give me a pep talk, try to talk me out of my feelings, and issue me assignments intended to work me out of my hurt.

And while I never doubted his heart for me, these efforts only seemed to add to my feelings of hurt. Despite his companionship and concern, they also compounded my feeling of loneliness. When I expressed this to him, he struggled to understand why. I was young then and didn't have adequate words to explain, but I basically said, "I don't want you to fix it. I just want you to listen and agree with me that this stinks."

Maybe I was wrong. Maybe I was disobedient not to simply obey his exhortations to improvement. Maybe I was lazy—actually, I probably was—or maybe I was too weirdly committed to feeling like a victim. Looking back, I'm sure I spent too much time feeling sorry for myself. But I also think I was learning something then about what it means to counsel and to comfort. In my own ministry to hurting people, I've doled out a wealth of well-intentioned words aimed at their feeling better, getting better, being better. But the deepest ministry of Jesus through my awkward efforts seems to always take place in the moments when I share someone's pain, agree with them that "this stinks," and set aside, even just temporarily, the spiritual Band-Aids in my pastoral toolkit.

You don't have to be alone to feel alone. I've learned this from the perpetrator's side of it, as well. I've been married for almost thirty years now, and I know I've made my wife feel achingly alone even when I've been nearby. When I rush to fix something she's shared with me without truly hearing her. When I withdraw from her because her hurt feels too inscrutable or just too inconvenient to me. In moments like those, somehow my being in the house makes her feel more alone than if I wasn't.

Obviously sometimes we do just need a good kick in the pants. Jesus can give us that too. He's perfectly capable of getting in our face, sternly but lovingly saying, "Hey, you: just snap out of it." But when we do that to others, very often we're saying something more about ourselves than we are the object of our admonitions. We're not usually reacting to someone's hurt or loneliness but to how that hurt or loneliness makes *us* feel. I know I have a tendency to be short with people I find "high maintenance." Maybe you do too.

Or maybe you've been on the receiving end of such impatient encouragement. I know I have. The good news is, we aren't high maintenance to Jesus.

When you thank Jesus for shouldering the weight of your life, and he says, "No problem," he means it. Nothing has ever been a problem to him. He'll never pull away from us, irritated by the inconvenience of us. He'll never ghost us, put out by the baggage we carry. He is perfectly present with us, and always so.

The Paraclete

John 5 tells the heartbreaking story of a disabled man desperate for help. There was a pool in Jerusalem where the sick and disabled were often brought. Perhaps the waters were thought to have healing properties. Perhaps it was just a place of refreshment and cleansing. In any event, there are a large number of physically needy people there. This poor fellow has been dealing with his disability for thirty-eight years. That's a long time to suffer.

But what hurts my heart more every time I read this passage is his experience at the pool. He describes being unable to enter the waters. Nobody will help him. "I have no one," he says (v. 7). When he tries to make his way into the waters by himself, others push around him, step over him, and prevent him from getting in.

Then Jesus shows up. We're told Jesus can see the man has been lying there for a very long time (v. 6). And, of course, the mercy of Christ proves miraculous for this man, who is instantly healed from his disability.

But I'm still struck by that long sentence of loneliness the man was serving. Hurt and despondent, he's been the victim of neglect and rough treatment for nearly forty years. Around the crowded pool, he's left to fend for himself while others take advantage of his disability. He's not alone, but he is. He is very, very alone.

I think of what might have happened to this man if Jesus didn't make that stop in his workday at Bethesda. What if Jesus prioritized some other ministry objective that day, maybe even someone else's healing? I mean, Jesus didn't heal everybody in Palestine. Some people were disabled before he began his earthly ministry and were still disabled when it was complete. What if this man had been one of them?

He'd remain lying there in his pain and uncleanliness for perhaps a few years more. Maybe he would die from neglect. Maybe he would die of loneliness. And if Jesus is too busy healing somebody else that day, would it be Jesus's fault? (While he's healing this man, there are still many others on the other side of town going without!) Jesus can't be everywhere at once.

Or can he?

When we fast-forward in John's Gospel to chapter 16, Jesus is speaking to his disciples about the impending completion of his earthly ministry.

Nevertheless, I am telling you the truth. It is for your benefit that I go away, because if I don't go away the Counselor will not come to you. If I go, I will send him to you. . . . When the Spirit of truth comes, he will guide you into all the truth. For he will not speak on his own, but he will speak whatever he hears. He will also declare to you what is to come. He will glorify me, because he will take from what is mine and declare it to you. (vv. 7, 13–14)

Jesus is saying it's better for the disciples if he goes away. He's referring to his future ascension, the moment some time after his resurrection when he'll return to the place from which he came. The disciples, naturally, will be saddened by this moment. They'll have gone through the trauma of their friend's crucifixion and then the elation of his glorious return, only for him to bid farewell to them again. How could he describe this turn of events as being to their advantage?

The answer speaks to the "problem" of some receiving Christ's personal touch during his ministry while others do not. In his incarnation, Jesus enters the physicality of space-time. The disciples cannot each enjoy his personal attention simultaneously. In the flesh, he cannot be present with every believer at once. But his omnipresence is brought to bear in the sending of the Holy Spirit.

Now, the Third Person of the Trinity is no less omnipresent than the Son. The Spirit has always been with God's people. But there's a special anointing, an official inauguration of the Spirit's ministry, just as Jesus promised, in Acts 2. While the Spirit has always been with worshipers of God in the way one has access to a steady flowing stream or a constantly blowing breeze, in Acts 2 the Spirit comes upon them like raging waters through a broken dam or the gale-force winds of a hurricane. This is how the incarnate Christ, now ascended, can continue to be with all of his brothers and sisters beyond the constraints of our four dimensions.

Jesus in John 16:7 calls the Holy Spirit "the Counselor." He is alternately referred to as our Comforter. The Greek word ascribed to the Spirit is *Paraclete*, which means "Helper." This is who the Spirit is, and this is what the Spirit does—help.

Because Christians have been baptized in the Holy Spirit, we can never be alone. Even when we're alone, we aren't truly alone. Even when we feel alone, we aren't truly alone.

In Matthew 6:6, Jesus instructs his disciples to forgo showy spirituality and to pray in secret. There's no need to make a big performance out of our spirituality in specially designated spaces of formal religion. We can pray in secret, Jesus says, because God "is in secret." The Spirit of Christ knows us and sees us and hears us and receives us.

Under the old covenant, if one wanted to bask in the presence of God, they'd need to attend to the rituals of the temple. That's where God was known to specially dwell. But because of Christ's atoning work, the dividing wall between sinners and the holiest place has been torn down (Mark 15:38), and the Spirit has now streamed out of buildings made by human hands and into human hearts (Ezek. 36:26; Eph. 3:17). Paul writes in Titus 3:6, "He poured out his Spirit on us abundantly through Jesus Christ our Savior." Our bodies are now his temple (1 Cor. 3:16; 6:19).

As the Spirit takes up residence in the hearts of believers in Christ, he grows in us the fruit of the Spirit (Gal. 5:22–25), which is the quality of Christlikeness. When we ponder the fruit of the Spirit, we ponder the character of Jesus. He is love, joy, peace, patience, kindness, goodness, faithfulness, gentleness, and self-control. The Spirit, through progressive sanctification, is imprinting on us the resemblance of Christ. This is part of how we become new through closeness with Jesus. The Holy Spirit gets close enough to indwell our souls (Rom. 8:2), and he is day by day renewing our inner selves (2 Cor. 4:16).

This closeness to Christ through his Spirit is making us into new people. Our thought life is changing. Our emotional life is changing. We are "growing up," so to speak, into the stature of Christ, into true spiritual maturity (Eph. 4:13). And this spiritual maturity fosters emotional maturity. The closer we get to Christ by his Spirit, the more conformed to Christ's image we become, the more able we are to regulate our emotions and engage in self-awareness, humility, peace-ability, and reasonableness. The fruit of the Spirit is real and transformative, and he is changing us into the people we ought to be, the people we long to be.

If we're honest with ourselves, we'll admit we desperately need the Helper's help. We need his counsel to discern matters of conscience and instances of delusion. Our flesh wars against us, but with the Spirit's power, we can wage war back. We need the conviction of sin he brings, even after we're saved, because we easily delude ourselves with false humility and hypocrisy and defensiveness.

For example, one of the easiest ways to become worldly without realizing it is to engage in religious concerns from the flesh. We justify derision and bitterness and scoffing, all things the Bible forbids, by claiming to defend Jesus and his gospel. You and I have to be very careful with the spirit of anger.

Many Christians who lose the battle against the flesh in the arena of anger do so because they imagine they're being prophetic or "contending for the faith" or even following the example of Jesus himself. After all, doesn't he drive the moneychangers from the temple with a whip and a barrage of curses? Doesn't he pronounce woes and condemnations?

But our anger isn't exactly like Jesus's anger. His indignation comes sparingly, as an exclamation point on a ministry otherwise characterized by peace. Jesus doesn't get out of bed looking to give sinners a kick in the pants. He does get out of bed looking to give the devil a swift kick! So Paul warns us that our warfare is "not of the flesh" (2 Cor. 10:4) and our fight isn't "against flesh and blood" (Eph. 6:12). Indeed, from the very mouth of Jesus, we are told not to attack our enemies but to love them (Matt. 5:44). That's how we demonstrate we belong to God.

Further, Jesus's anger is always righteous. It is never corrupted or influenced by sin, for Jesus is sinless. We are not. Thus, there are far too many warnings about anger in the Bible for us to engage in it cavalierly. It is for these reasons that under-shepherds, as pastoral signposts to the Good Shepherd, must not be hot-tempered (Titus 1:7) or quarrelsome (1 Tim. 3:3). Jesus was not a bully.

Some of the biggest jerks I've known have been pastors. And some of the best friends I've known have been pastors. I think both experiences are true for the same reason: pastors are especially burdened by the sin and brokenness of God's people. They see more of it in the church and know it more intimately than the laity. For some, this knowledge hardens them, callousing their hearts, making them rougher than they ought to be. But for others, this knowledge softens them, making them more tender. The latter is the way of Christ.

To give in to anger, then, to be short-tempered, is to misinterpret the wrath of Christ as his normative disposition. Every Christian, pastor or not, must always be eager for peace (Heb. 12:14), because Jesus is. Apart from him, we cannot manage any of this. But the Spirit gives us the growing power of self-control. And as he bears more and more in us the fruit of Christlikeness, we leave the impression of our Savior more and more with those around us.

With the help of the Holy Spirit, we can know Christ and make him known. We can be ever near to him and give others the sense of his nearness. And as Christ draws near to sinners like us, by his Spirit we can draw near even to sinners *not* like us. In the flesh, this closeness is impossible. But with Christ, all things are possible.

Christians bring the ministry of the Helper with them wherever they go. For many, the way of Jesus seems like a fairy tale, some kind of religious urban legend. Oh, they've heard the stories. They see spiritual leaders on cable news or social media making big claims about Jesus. But it sounds too good to be true. Many—for good reason—suspect the goodness of Christ among Christians is all talk and no action. Jesus's presence died with Jesus, they conclude.

But then real Christians come near. In the Spirit of Christ, they minister to the least, the last, and the lost, and the gears of imagination begin to turn. The Spirit enables every Christian to become a walking apologetic for the Good News. *Maybe this Jesus is real*, an onlooker thinks. *Maybe he really is present. And maybe, just maybe, he actually loves me.*

When a person encounters the Spirit of Christ, they have encountered Christ.

I imagine that previously disabled man at the Bethesda pool could "Amen" Job's declaration, which he issues at the conclusion of his own touching encounter with God: "I had heard reports about you, but now my eyes have seen you" (Job 42:5).

Does Job literally behold the Son of God? Perhaps. But more likely, as God speaks to him by the Spirit, drawing near to his affliction and lifting him up into the dizzying splendor of the Lord's own sovereign glory, Job truly feels he has. Through his suffering and the closeness of God's Spirit with him in it, his belief goes from audio to video. This is life with the divine Helper.

The Spirit reveals Christ to us. Our Paraclete helps us to see Christ, to sense Christ's presence in our lowest moments, in the deepest of pits, in our loneliest of loneliness. And he helps us know Christ's presence in the presence of his brothers and sisters.

In the physical absence of Jesus, in this time between his first and second comings, the spiritual body of Christ, formed and filled by the Spirit, is comprised of the people at all our Bethesda pools who will fulfill the law of Christ. We're the ones who prove no one need be alone. We're the crowd who will help a body into the water.

The Body of Christ

It was the last Sunday of my pastorate. With a trembling voice, I managed to preach through Genesis 22 and make it to the closing of the service without breaking down. It was a difficult day for me, made more difficult by the overwhelming feeling of unfinished business in my ministry. Resigning had been disorienting for me. To be fair, it had been fairly disorienting for many in my church as well. There didn't seem to be a clear reason, to them, why I would call it quits. They did not all understand why I would want to leave. The church, by all accounts, was doing well. We had been growing very well for a few years. We were making significant inroads into local mission, including developing a local church plant. People enjoyed my preaching. We had developed vibrant ministries of benevolence and programs of fellowship.

So it startled people when I submitted my resignation. You're supposed to quit when you've failed! You don't quit when things are going well. Still, success is not an excuse for disobeying God. And while discerning God's strange call to move my ministry elsewhere was a daunting thing, I knew it would be more dangerous to disregard it.

As I took to the pulpit for the last time, I wasn't sure how things were going to go. For a long time, I had felt alone. There were many in the church who misunderstood my resignation. Afterward, there were a few who criticized me and still more who accused me of all kinds of things, none of them true. I chalked up most of them to anger about my leaving and disappointment in me. But trying to understand my critics didn't make me feel less alone. When I turned the corner from the closing prayer to the closing hymn, despite believing a shore of safety lay in my future, I still felt adrift.

And then something remarkable happened. I stood on the little stage of that little country church, all by my lonesome, as the congregation sang my favorite hymn, "And Can It Be," and suddenly I sensed action all around me. A group of men bounded up onto the stage to join me. They didn't want me to finish alone. They encircled me, laying their hands on my shoulders and back, and sang loudly alongside me.

I felt as though I could be raptured up into heaven at that moment.

At its best, the church embodies the felt presence of Christ. I know from experience, as you may too, that being surrounded by church people can be a quite lonely experience. But I also know, with the Spirit's help, that it can be a ministry to us of Christ himself. He has promised to be with us, and he keeps this promise through the Spirit-birthed church.

There's a reason the New Testament refers to the church as the body of Christ (1 Cor. 12:27). It isn't simply about the organization of gifts, or even the fact that together we're a living organism. It's because Jesus has grafted us together into himself. With his atoning work, he hasn't just reconciled us individually to God but corporately, in God, to each other.

In Romans 12:5, Paul writes that "we who are many are one body in Christ and individually members of one another." The communion of the saints is possible only through the saints' mystical union with Jesus. Unified through the gospel, we aren't adherents to the same ideology or patrons of the same club. We are "members of one another."

This is why the concept of church membership is so important. The details may vary from tradition to tradition, church to church, but the basis of church membership is found in the covenantal reality of life in Christ. The Spirit is making a heavenly family. And the local church is an embassy of that heaven, a "family home" for a collection of believers baptized into Christ and into the community of his new covenant.

I know church gets weird. I know church members get weird. But we're weird too. And in the same way Jesus tolerates our weirdness, accepting us on the basis of our faith, we ought to strive to extend the same grace to others. The local church is the great laboratory of grace, where we put to the test our mutual adherence to the Good News. Do we believe that forgiveness is real? Do we believe that confession is the doorway to pardon? Do we believe that Jesus won't turn away anyone who comes to him? Then let us prove it by our commitment to the church. Let's prove it by our commitment to *a* church.

As we practice the variety of New Testament "one anothers" and observe the church's ordinances, we get to experience the changing closeness of Jesus. This isn't just about identifying with a tradition or embracing a religion. It's about surrendering our self-interest and crucifying our self-centeredness to follow the Savior.

In our world, we've been accustomed to church as production, as attraction. We "go to church" without finding much necessity in *being* the church, because the consumeristic and pragmatic values of the world have overwhelmed our spiritual sensing of our need for Jesus. We feel instead the need for inspiration, for moral uplift, for—honestly—entertainment. These are all terrible alternatives to experiencing the presence of Christ, but they tick all the boxes of our felt needs and fleshly instincts, so we happily accept them. A family goes to church expecting an experience, to be sure, and they imagine themselves satisfied when the music is sufficiently emotive and the teaching sufficiently inspirational. But later they still feel as if something is missing, because despite the emotion and inspiration, they haven't experienced Jesus at the primary place designed for that experience.

We can make do with emotion and inspiration when times are relatively easy, perhaps even when occasionally challenging. But when life goes off the rails, when we're sitting in the ash heap of a life in ruin, they're cold comfort. I know, because I've been there. It happened to me while I was part of a church that centered an "experience" over the experience of Christ. And it left me practically unable to cope with the wreckage I had wrought.

And yet, Jesus still came near.

The church aware of her identity as the body of Christ has been endowed with the Spirit with all the power and all the gifts necessary to help us see Jesus magnified in our vision. The church aware of her identity as the body of Christ sings, prays, preaches, and serves with such capital *S* Spiritual force that, even when she doesn't "feel it," she's sharing in the very heart of her namesake.

Jesus so wants us to understand this that he places his identity in the center of our identity. When we love each other, we're loving him. When we serve each other, we're serving him. The whole ecclesiological enterprise is set up so that when we forget platform and repent of our positioning, even service to the person in the church with the least social currency is a service unto Christ (Matt. 25:40). Thus his magnificent kingdom comes to bear in our ordinary, messy, little churches.

We rob ourselves of this relational proximity to Jesus when we disobey his command to "one another" each other. When the author of Hebrews tells us not to neglect gathering together (10:24–25), it's not because going to church is some sign of religious superiority but because he wants us to know the intimacy of "a new and living way through the curtain"

(v. 20). When we don't just go to church but join a church, assuming our responsibility as a vital member of his body, we "enter the sanctuary through the blood of Jesus" (v. 19).

Therefore, to say (in so many words) about the church, "I don't need you!" (1 Cor. 12:21) is to say to Jesus, "I don't need you."

But we do need him.

The biblical ordinances of baptism and communion are indicators of this. When we observe a baptism, we're observing someone choosing life! To turn from sin and profess faith in Jesus through the baptismal waters is to announce that we need Jesus in order to really live. And when we observe the Lord's Supper, we're admitting we don't live by bread alone. We need the sustenance of Christ.

Just as the old covenant community was identified by its markers of circumcision and Passover observance, the new covenant community is identified by its own markers. Baptism and communion show that we belong to Jesus and that, in fact, he's present with us. When properly discerned, they're visible reminders to us that we aren't merely religiously observant but relationally bound—to God and, through him, to each other. The ordinances remind us over and over again of the covenant Jesus has made with his bride. He has given her his very body.

The Covenant

As the hymn goes, "Friends may fail me; foes assail me. He, my Savior, makes me whole."[2] If you've ever wondered, as we pondered in chapter 1, "Where did everybody go?" you're not alone. That truth alone should be of some comfort!

The dreadful feeling of loneliness is part and parcel with the human condition. Jesus himself experiences it when his closest friends abandon him. Every great hero of the faith has endured a harrowing sense of abandonment. If you struggle with this feeling even this moment, take at least some encouragement in knowing your experience is common even among those the Lord loves.

The greater encouragement, however, is in knowing who will reliably never leave us alone. "At my first defense," Paul writes, "no one stood by me, but everyone deserted me. May it not be counted against them. But the Lord stood with me and strengthened me" (2 Tim. 4:16–17). However we feel, we can know, as we've seen previously, that the Lord is closer than our skin!

One of the prevailing images of Christ's commitment to us that we see in both the Old and New Testaments is that of the marital covenant. In the New Testament, the church is referred to as the bride of Christ because of the nature of his faithfulness—and closeness—to us. A married couple is said to become "one flesh" (Gen. 2:24), and this beautiful enfleshed-ness becomes a picture of the believer's union with Christ.

Now, of course, our marriages aren't perfect. The divorce rate alone is proof enough of that. But even among marriages that never split up, we can experience hurt and loneliness of all kinds. When we marry, we marry a sinner. (And the person we marry does too.) Still, the marriage between a man and a woman is best viewed in covenantal terms. We often speak of the "marriage contract," but a contract isn't the best category for what a marriage, biblically speaking, is meant to be. A contract is a legal agreement with terms.

Once the terms are violated, by either party, the contract is broken. The marriage is broken.

Within a covenant, however, we agree to an enduring faithfulness regardless of contractual terms. This is why we vow at our marriage ceremonies to stay committed "for better or worse." Entering a covenant is our way of saying, "I will be unilaterally faithful. My faithfulness to you isn't contingent upon the best circumstances. I pledge my loyalty to you out of grace." This doesn't mean that there aren't biblically allowable grounds for divorce, but every divorce, even if justifiable, is a tragedy. Covenants aren't made to be broken.

This covenantal vision reflects the gospel (Eph. 5:31–32). The work of salvation is the unilateral, gracious commitment Christ makes to a sinner. He knows full well we will fail him daily. He knows full well we'll be unfaithful, that we'll essentially cheat on him every day. He sees all this going into the relationship, but he stands at the altar with us and, when presented with the prospect of taking us sinners as his bride, he resolutely says, "I do."

The union Jesus makes with us is covenantally perfect. While we will struggle to maintain our end of the relationship, he's unflagging and unfailing. He will be faithful. The covenant endures because he endures.

Jesus will never divorce his bride. He'll never abandon her. Consider these promises, straight from the Lord's mouth:

"I will not leave you as orphans." (John 14:18)

"I will never leave you or abandon you." (Heb. 13:5)

"I am with you always." (Matt. 28:20)

"No one will snatch them out of my hand." (John 10:28)

He remains close to us always. He isn't just a faithful husband but a faithfully loving and affectionate husband. His desire for us isn't simply to be aware of his proximity but to be affected by his enduring presence.

The early church father Athanasius once asked, "For what profit would there be for those who were made, if they did not know their own Maker?"[3] Indeed. We were made for this closeness, for this intimacy. Why would he have made you otherwise?

Do you desire closeness with Jesus? You can know that he desires closeness with you. He couldn't have done anything more to prove it. "The LORD is with you when you are with him. If you seek him, he will be found by you" (2 Chron. 15:2).

Do you feel lonely? He hasn't abandoned those who seek him (Ps. 9:10). Do you feel hopeless? He protects those who hope in his Word (119:114). Do you feel lost? Jesus has come to seek *you* and to save you (Luke 19:10).

The Pigsty

Imagine with me, if you will, an alternate version of the parable of the prodigal son. I suspect we are meant to envision this scenario, considering what's left unsaid and undone in the parable as Jesus tells it. Imagine you are that rebellious child, and you turn on your father and go off on your own way.

The living is good for a while. Or so you think. You're spending the father's grace like crazy. But every party has to end. Maybe you find it at the bottom of the empty barrel of drugs and alcohol. Maybe you find it in the lonely

191

bed of sexual immorality. Maybe you find it in the spiritual bankruptcy of theological heresy. Whatever it was your heart yearned for that wasn't worthy of God, you spent all your time and energy on it and came out on the other end with nothing to show for it but a deeper ache and, worse, the devastating realization that you're far from home, where the one you have forsaken now lives without you.

You have no idea how to get back. You don't even see how you could show your face there. For all intents and purposes, that life is over. Done. Demolished. There's no going back.

One morning, tired of your behavior, tired of your life, and tired of *yourself*, you drag yourself to the front stoop of the dingy shack that's your new lot in life. You plop yourself down and put your face in your hands. *I've blown it*, you think.

It doesn't last long, though, because you figure if you're this far gone, you might as well keep going. If there's no going back, maybe you should just go on and throw it all away. The shell that remains of your soul is plunged into the mire of despair. You're in with the pigs now. Your life is such a disaster, your insides so empty, you look with hunger at the slop around you. You know it's what you deserve.

This is where you have come to die. Oh, maybe not physically. Not for a while. But you may as well, because something in you has died already. It's a living death. And each day is the same as the one before. The cancer of insignificance begins to eat you up inside. You are a forgotten speck of nothingness on the face of a colossal, uncaring earth.

Do you feel it?

Now, imagine you're sitting in that dung-poisoned mud, and you bring yourself to glance up at the horizon. You see the figure of a man on the horizon. He is getting closer, coming toward you. The last thing you want now that you feel utterly alone is to have someone close by! It seems someone is coming along to see the mess you've made of yourself.

As the man nears your pen, you see it's not a stranger. It's your older brother. In this version of the story, your brother is not a judgmental weirdo. He's the best guy you've ever known. You've imagined that, as you've blown through your father's generosity, he's been filling Dad's ear with all the ways you're a screwup who doesn't deserve any help. You know deep down your brother's not like that, but you know that's the kind of brother you deserve.

He's opening the gate now and stepping into the pigsty. His nice shoes are getting sloppy. He sloshes his way near to stand over you. Bracing yourself, you're expecting a lecture. That's the last thing you want. *Just kill me*, you think. But to your surprise, he hitches up his pants and sits down next to you.

He puts his hand on your shoulder.

You thought you were all cried out, but through the dryness, through the redness, your eyes begin to well up. You don't know what to say. He could be sitting back at home, next to a roaring fire, enjoying Dad's food, surrounded by Dad's comfort. He could've spent the rest of his life just wondering what became of you.

Instead, he came looking for you.

You turn meekly to him and say, "Why?"

And he says, "I just didn't want you to be alone."

He has come to keep covenant with you. There is no friend so perfectly present as Jesus.

10

I Love You to Death

(Jesus the Saving Friend)

D'ye know what Calvary was? What? What? What? . . .
It was *damnation*; and he took it *lovingly*.

John Duncan[1]

There is no friend so saving as Jesus. His love for us isn't
mere sentiment. He isn't merely inclined toward us. The
love of Jesus is no simple fondness. Jesus is all in with his
care for us. And he was and is always willing to show it.

As we journey through Old Testament history, it's astonishing just how faithful God remains to his people. He has
set them apart and set his favor on them. He gives them an
identity, a culture, a purpose. He gives them his very presence. He delivers them miraculously time after time. And

every day, for thousands of years, they flirt with sin and indulge in idol worship. Yet he never leaves them. His loving-kindness is as persistent as their waywardness.

When we get to the New Testament, Jesus begins calling his disciples, twelve in number as a symbolic continuity with the twelve tribes of Israel, and he's consciously and explicitly recruiting men of low reputation. Onto the ship of redemption he brings aboard tax collectors, despised members of society seen as traitorous to his Jewish brethren. He welcomes zealots and hotheads, the very kind of people who could put his kingdom movement at risk. And instead of bringing in religious scholars or spiritual authorities, he calls fishermen, just regular blue-collar Joes. On the surface, it would seem he's designing his mission to fail.

These are misfit friends. They don't always get along with each other. They don't always get along with *him*! And as he leads, they question him, misunderstand him, misinterpret him, and misjudge him. Still, he keeps bringing them along. There's no explanation except that he must really love these guys.

There is no explanation except that he must plan to demonstrate what real love *is*. Not simply a feeling but something deeper. Something not rooted in human emotions or romantic reciprocation. Real love is a unilateral commitment to a person's good despite that person's badness. Real love is rooted in a divine forbearance.

We're so sinful that we struggle to sacrifice for the good of people who actually do good to us. How far from our minds, then, is the idea of sacrificing for somebody evil? The apostle Paul wrestles with this very truth in Romans 5:7, when he talks about how rare it is for someone to sacrifice themselves for a righteous person. He admits that occasionally someone might "dare to die" for a good person. Sacrificial living even among the good is a rarity. Knowing this, it's an amazing turn of events that Christ would die for us "while we were still sinners" (v. 8).

Their three-year apprenticeship to Jesus is undeniably sanctifying, but as this motley crew bumbles their way closer to Golgotha, they're still nowhere near a position of deserving what's about to happen. And when the time comes to pay the ultimate price for these losers, Jesus, the very embodiment of love, goes willingly, resolutely, lovingly to pay it. He does it—get this—*for joy* (Heb. 12:2).

Jesus tells his followers, "No one has greater love than this: to lay down his life for his friends" (John 15:13), and he isn't blowing smoke. What they won't do for him, at least not at the time, he will still do for them.

What we *could not* do for him, he does for us.

Proverbs 18:24 tells us that "there is a friend who stays closer than a brother." Jesus is that friend.

He's the friend who "loves at all times" (17:17), which includes, of course, the times that are painful, the times that are crucial, the times that are costly. Jesus is the friend who, when your life is on the line, will pick up that line for you.

A Life Laid Down

One day, a prophet leaves his brother in charge of the family while he goes up a mountain to have an appointment with God. It's a long, detailed meeting—forty days and forty nights in all—and apparently that's just the right amount of time for the family to absolutely lose their minds. When the prophet finally returns home, he finds that everybody is out of control (Exod. 32:25).

The prophet's name is Moses. His brother is Aaron. And the family might as well be called idiots, because despite having personally experienced one miraculous deliverance after another from the mighty hand of YHWH, they let Moses's delay get them just antsy enough to melt all their jewelry down, mold it into a calf, and worship it as a god.

It's the exact kind of thing the true God has forbidden, and explicitly so. And it's the exact kind of forbidden thing that would merit a smiting from the same. Aaron knows this is just absolute deadly craziness, but he tries to cover up the family's idolatry by building an altar in front of the calf and announcing a festival to God. As if God would be fooled by such a ploy.

But God notices. He notices everything. And he literally interrupts the meeting he's having with Moses on top of Mount Sinai to basically say, "Hold up. This just in. Your brothers and sisters have gone completely off the rails." God orders Moses to descend the mountain and sort things out. In the meantime, he says, "I'm going to burn against them and wipe them out."

Now, he assures Moses that he's still going to make a mighty nation out of the man, even if he kills everybody else. So Moses knows that he would still have the Lord's favor even if he lost all of his countrymen. But a curious thing happens. Moses intercedes for his idiot people anyway. He pleads with God to spare the Israelites total destruction, and God agrees.

But it gets deeper. After Moses returns home and sees the rampant idolatry for himself (and Aaron's lame excuses for it), he orders a measured dose of God's wrath: the death penalty for three thousand men. And with the remnant of men left, still realizing that God's wrath may not be satisfied, Moses offers to make atonement.

He asks God to forgive his brothers. But Moses knows forgiveness comes at a price. So he offers up himself. "Please erase me from the book you have written," he says (v. 32). Moses is willing to receive God's wrath in exchange for sparing the remaining members of his family. And he doesn't do that because he's happy with them!

We find the apostle Paul writing in a similar vein in Romans 9:3, when he says he wishes he could be "cursed and cut off" for the benefit of his Jewish brethren who have rejected Jesus. He wants them to know the saving love of Jesus so much, he's willing to forgo it himself, if that's what it would take.

Now, it doesn't take the death of Moses or Paul for God's people to know the saving love of Christ. But it does take the death of Christ. And the heart of these two men for the sake of their friends is a reflection of Christ's own sacrificial heart. As Paul says, it is barely possible that someone would lay their life down for someone who deserved it. But for somebody who *didn't* deserve it? For somebody who deserved to give up their own life? Who would sacrifice themselves for that kind of person? It's like you or I suddenly appeared in that darkened room in Abbottabad, Pakistan, right as Seal Team 6 breached the door to bring justice to Osama bin Laden, and cried out, "Don't kill him! Kill me instead."

And if you think that illustration is a little extreme, you don't know the severity of your sin against a holy God. That you're breathing right now, at least enough to read this book, is an immense gift of grace. God is holy and we are not.

He is also merciful in a way that we aren't. His mercy overflows heaven and spills onto earth. It fills the womb of a virgin. It fills the earth with the emptying of itself. The incarnation of the Son is itself a stunning example of his life laid down. He, in a sense, lays himself down from heaven to earth. He stoops from his heavenly throne to make his home among sinners. While he at all times maintains his deity—the whole fullness of it (Col. 2:9)—he never pulls the ripcord to the divine parachute. The God of the universe gets low.

When Paul exhorts us to lay our own lives down for the sake of others, to embrace humility and servant-hearted sacrifice, he doesn't motivate us with high-minded ideals of human virtue or religious merit. No, he points to the example of our friend Jesus:

> Do nothing out of selfish ambition or conceit, but in humility consider others as more important than yourselves. Everyone should look not to his own interests, but rather to the interests of others.
>
> Adopt the same attitude as that of Christ Jesus,
>
> > who, existing in the form of God,
> > did not consider equality with God
> > as something to be exploited.
> > Instead he emptied himself
> > by assuming the form of a servant,
> > taking on the likeness of humanity.
> > And when he had come as a man,
> > he humbled himself by becoming obedient
> > to the point of death—
> > even to death on a cross. (Phil. 2:3–8)

There is no friend so humble as Jesus! The King of kings and Lord of lords empties himself and humbles himself. He loves his friends so much he lays down his very life for us. Jesus's love is a self-emptying love, a love so deep it will seek the glory of others even if doing so requires the abasement of itself.

A Love Torn Up

The first question I ask couples in the course of premarital counseling is, "Why do you want to get married?" I've heard a number of responses to that question, but none as surprising as that from one bride-to-be at my last church.

The answer I get is usually some variation of "because we're in love," and that's fine as far as that goes. I'm glad they're in love! I'd be a little concerned if they weren't. But I use answers like that to point couples to the gospel as the grounding of their relationship. The love of Jesus perseveres when our love fails, so it's a much greater foundation for marriage. But this young lady cut right to the chase.

I asked, "Why do you want to be married?"

She said, "I think it would be more sanctifying than being single."

I might have spit out my coffee.

Once I regained my bearings and asked her to repeat herself, I then asked her to elaborate. She said, "Well, I know myself well enough to know that I'm a very selfish person. I lived for a little bit with my brother when he moved to town and needed a place to stay, and I discovered how even just living with a family member exposed things in my heart and life that I need to surrender to God. So I think being married will have to be more sanctifying for me than staying single."

It obviously wasn't the most romantic answer I'd ever heard. I looked over at her fiancé. He just shrugged. But he also smiled. And I did too. As they were members of my church, I knew this couple well, and I knew that they were both strong believers with very mature faith. They'd found each other in the notoriously unreliable world of online matchmaking by intentionally looking for a potential partner committed to radical discipleship to Jesus. This young lady's fiancé was a guy totally sold out for Christ, an active street evangelist, and a prospective elder at our church. So he wasn't put off by her answer at all. He probably thought her "sanctification" response was the hottest thing he could've heard!

Years later, I still think about this exchange. To say one wants to marry because they know it will be more sanctifying than not being married is essentially to say, "I want to be willing to embrace any circumstance that promises to make me more like Jesus." I'm still impressed by this attitude, wherever I find it. Among those suffering with lifelong disabilities or from life-ending diseases. Among men and women who commit to leave the comfort and safety of their homes to minister the gospel in some very hostile places. Among those battling anxiety or depression. Anyone who can legitimately say, "I'm willing to undergo whatever it takes to conform my life to Christ" is hugely impressive to me.

And over the years, what I've discovered is that those most willing to say that are those who most understand that Christ was willing to do so for them. Marriage isn't easy, but compared to what Jesus has endured for our sakes, committing it to the consecration of the gospel is a piece of cake. The amount of human suffering a soul can endure is indeed tremendous. But in the light of the cross, it can be a glorious sharing in the afflictions of Christ (Phil. 3:10; Col. 1:24).

To some, this idea sounds awful, like a martyr's complex or worse. I want to be clear that this approach to seeing all things in the light of Christ's sacrifice isn't about enjoying pain or faking strength or any other twisted thing. It's simply about trusting God to steer all things toward our eternal good and conformity to the image of Jesus.

When that young lady categorized marriage in her heart as sanctifying unto Christ, she was saying to her future husband, "Whatever it costs, I'm with you." Because that's exactly what Christ has said to us.

Coming to the end of his journey with the twelve disciples, Jesus faces an agonizing test in the garden of Gethsemane. Would he press on, enduring what lay ahead, for these men? "He fell facedown and prayed, 'My Father, if it is possible, let this cup pass from me. Yet not as I will, but as you will'" (Matt. 26:39).

How do we know the love of Jesus isn't mere sentiment? Because it stands between us and the full force of the hellish wrath of God. Love drinks from the cup of judgment that we might drink of joy.

The cross is a symbol of that intersection: wrath and mercy. There Jesus receives from God the punishment of sin we deserve while pouring out with his own blood the grace we don't. But the cross wasn't a symbol—at least, not at first. The cross was a real thing. It was a real thing that real human bodies were tied to, nailed through the hands and feet to, lifted up on, and displayed upon. He came in love, *as love*, and we tore him up.

I don't know how you picture hell. It certainly isn't like the stupid cartoon depictions we see in the movies and on the television. The biblical portraits are horrifying. It's the place of simultaneous darkness and blazing fire. It's a place of both destruction and conscious torment. It's the place of God's active presence (in wrath) and yet full of the devastating sense of his absence. There's a reason we call the worst things we can imagine "hell."

But hell is worse than we can imagine. So when we look more deeply into what Jesus is willing to endure for sinners, we can begin to more fully see he bears on his very body the reality of hell. He is cursed at, spit on, and beaten. He's stripped naked into shame and whipped viciously into tatters. A wreath of hard thorns is screwed onto his head. Nails are hammered through his flesh into the wood of the beams. He is hung up for all to see.

As he is spent, gaunt, and dying, the onlookers gape at his shame. Strips of skin dangle in bloody flaps from his body, but they desecrate him further. A bitter sponge is raked across his raw lips. A spear is plunged into his side. If you didn't know it was Jesus, you wouldn't recognize him.

Surely he could have come up with some other way to save his friends. Surely there's some other means of demonstrating the greatness of his affection for us. But no. There's the holiness of God, and there's the fallenness of humankind, and ne'er the twain shall meet—except through the hands of Jesus. He gives us the great love of himself, and we murder him for it. But we have no idea he's winning us at the same time.

At the cross, love goes to hell and emerges victorious over it. It is damnation, as a man once said, and he takes it lovingly. He takes *us* lovingly too. There's no greater love a man can have for his friends than to lay down his life, have it torn up, and then have it *raised* up for their salvation.

Pondering the brutality of the cross, Jesus says, "I'll do that for you." Whatever it costs him, he loves you. He loves us to death.

A Life Made New

His love changes us. Jesus certainly has proven that he loves his friends just as they are, but he wouldn't love us much if he intended us to *stay* as we are. So through the power of his cross and resurrection, his Spirit begins to transform us into his likeness. We know this power better the more time we spend with Jesus. After a while, we cannot help but resemble him. We're becoming more like our true selves too, of course! We're becoming who we were meant to be, before the indwelling of sin and the invasion of brokenness. But we're simultaneously becoming more like Jesus. What a miracle his grace is!

In his presence, more and more, the old dies and the new grows. Outside we may be getting older, but inside we're getting younger. As his sanctifying presence administers grace to every corner of our hearts, we find the vestiges of death gradually stripped away, like flaking paint scraped from an old wall. We're being restored. The closer to him we get, the more we are renewed. By this, our glorious Savior makes his ugly friends beautiful.

The work of salvation is itself beautiful, because it's our beautiful Christ who is at work in it. It's beautiful, because it's an act of unilateral, effectual grace. "This is what the

Lord GOD says: It is not for your sake that I will act, house of Israel, but for my holy name" (Ezek. 36:22).

Who is the one acting? It is God.

He brings his glory to bear upon the helpless state of the fallen. For sinners in a state of spiritual death, he brings the rescue of his glorious life. Jesus's friends aren't people who simply need a leg up or a handout. No, we're dead and in bondage to sin, unable to save ourselves. On our own, "there is no one who seeks God" (Rom. 3:11). "The person without the Spirit does not receive what comes from God's Spirit, because it is foolishness to him; he is not able to understand it since it is evaluated spiritually" (1 Cor. 2:14). God alone is our only hope.

Salvation is all of grace, or it isn't salvation. Self-righteousness is gross. But God-wrought salvation is beautiful, because it reflects the glory of our beautiful Christ.

Salvation is beautiful in its design too. While the image of the cross is grotesque, what it effects for sinners is brilliant. For a sinner to take up their cross is a pleasing reflection of the gospel.

I have a friend who was born into a family with an alcoholic and verbally abusive father. He says flatly, "I hated my dad." Even at the age of six or seven, my friend wanted to get out of his house. He hated his life and hated himself because of it. Every day his father would be drunk and stumbling around the house, good for nothing. Every week, he drank whatever paycheck he happened to earn from the jobs he kept losing. And then there were no more jobs. The family became desperate for money, so they began to sell everything they could.

My friend says they sold most of their clothes, all their games and toys, appliances, anything that might bring a little bit of money into the home to buy them some more time. It was a miserable existence that only promised to get worse. And then one day a lady came to the house to buy my friend's pedal car for her own children. The lady was a Christian. And she began to talk to my friend's drunken dad about Jesus.

This man had never heard these things. He was told that Jesus loved him as he was, that Jesus wasn't waiting for him to clean himself up, that he could be forgiven just where he stood or sat or lay helplessly in the gutter. He was told that Jesus could make him new. And what do you know, my friend's dad gave his life to Christ.

My friend became a Christian because he saw his dad become a Christian. He told me, "I've never seen a transformation so total. Even though it sent him into a dangerous sickness of withdrawal, my dad instantly quit drinking and smoking. Even though he had a lot of medical challenges, he took the lead in our family for the first time, and he began to set an example in Bible reading and prayer. He began to disciple us. I know Jesus is true because I've seen how powerfully he can change somebody."

The old became gloriously new.

But while our eyes can behold people repenting and professing their faith in Christ, we cannot behold the eternal weight of glory leading up to this moment and flowing out of it. Not yet, anyway. What happens in salvation is beautiful, but we won't see the fullness of its beauty until we see our saving friend face-to-face.

"If anyone is in Christ, he is a new creation; the old has passed away, and see, the new has come!" (2 Cor. 5:17). And we will see. We'll see the one who loved us enough to go to his own death on our behalf. We'll see the one who loved us enough to bring us with him out of that grave. We'll see the one who loves us enough to intercede for us at the right hand of God forever. We'll see the one who's committed to our everlasting newness.

Receiving salvation isn't simply becoming religious. It's turning to the glory of Jesus, finding Jesus beautiful. And this turning is a gift of the Spirit that he himself gives us freely. We need the eyes of faith granted in the new birth to see him as glorious. And when we do see him, we *behold* him. In Christ, we lose taste for all of our other options; all the alternatives pale in comparison to his surpassing splendor.

I don't know about you, but I can't wait to see him. Like a lot of Christians, I look forward to the "everything else" of heaven—all the sights and sounds, the laughter and the joys, the wonders and the feasting—but most of all, far above it all, I anticipate looking into the eyes of my most faithful friend.

You should know that Jesus is the whole point of the heavenly realm. Ezekiel 48:35 says the very name of the place is "The Lord Is There."

When you get there, his beauty will beautify everything, including you. He'll have made good on his daily promise to make a brand-new you. And even though you'll be seeing his face for the first time, you won't meet as strangers. It'll be a reunion. It'll simply be the next day in a succession of days of friendship with Jesus, only this time eternally more so.

He'll come with a shout and the blast of a trumpet. In the twinkling of an eye, we will be transformed. He will meet us in the air. He will bring in the new heavens and the new earth. And it will be, for us, like walking into the next room. Why wouldn't close friends with Jesus be there?

We get a taste of this heaven now. He has put it into us by his Spirit upon our conversion. He nourishes it daily through our participation in the divine dialogue. When we slow down to be friends with Jesus, we are getting glimpses of what it means to be citizens of heaven (Phil. 3:20).

But the glimpses are so pale, aren't they? We've talked about this before, the invisibility thing. We have to walk by faith for now, not by sight. As exhilarating as friendship with Jesus can be on this fallen earth, the day of exaltation will outshine even these precious moments like the sun outshines a candle. One day our faith will be sight, and the one who laid his life down for us will lift us up to himself in glory. We will be as close as we could ever get. And we'll be changed.

He loved us to death. And he will love us to death. And through death. And beyond death, into the everlasting day where death isn't just a distant memory but a nonfactor, a nonentity, a zero, a nothing.

Each of us is getting older, slower, less and less fresh, to the point of getting gray and spotted. Eventually we'll sputter out, and they'll put our sorry carcass in a box in the ground. All the more reason to stay tight with the one who will walk through all of it with us. He has gone through it before us, and he'll see us through it all. Death won't have the last word. He will. He *is* the Word! So though we outwardly may be falling apart, inwardly our friend Jesus is making us newer every day.

He will make everything beautiful in its time (Eccles. 3:11), including you. Wouldn't you make time for that?

CONCLUSION

What is broken inside of you?

What have you identified as the missing piece from your life? How do you define that inconsolable longing that creeps up out of your heart, even in the happiest of circumstances, and reminds you you're still not whole?

Whatever you want to call it, whatever you think is the most major of your malfunctions, the consolation is undoubtedly to know Jesus as a real person. Being a religious person won't solve what's wrong with you. Deep down, you know that. You've tried it. It doesn't work. It may impress others, but it doesn't get to the root of who you really are.

And what you are is a sinner. Yes, you've got baggage. You've got "issues." You've got wounds and scars. We all do. Some of us are better at hiding them than others, but there's no escaping the curse of living in a fallen world. But the thing that supremely ails us, the thing you and I can do absolutely nothing about on our own, is that we're infected with rebellion. We all fall short of the glory of God.

But the good news is that the biggest problem we have, the problem of our very selves, is no problem at all for the God who loves us. And he so loves us that he's willing to unite himself to us.

Jesus enters the room. We're nervous because, well, *he's Jesus*. But he looks at us like we're just the person he wants to see. He draws near to us as if we're the only person on earth. That a person like him would want to be friends with someone like you and me—can you believe it?

What a friend he is. You've never had a friend like him.

Do you want a friend who's pure of heart? There's no friend truer than Jesus.

Do you want a friend who doesn't pretend? There's no friend so real as Jesus.

Do you want a friend who will stick by you at every moment, high and low? There's no friend closer than Jesus.

Do you want a friend who understands you when you're hurt, knows just what to say and what to do, and will just sit with you and comfort you? There's no friend so comforting as Jesus.

Do you want a friend who will embrace you and won't be scared off by the mess that is you? There is no friend so unbothered as Jesus.

Do you want a friend who won't betray you? No one's ever been more loyal than Jesus.

Do you want a friend who will shoot you straight, even when it hurts, though his plan is always to heal? There's no friend so honest as Jesus.

Do you want a friend who won't leave you in the lurch, who will never leave you empty-handed or empty-hearted? There's no friend so generous as Jesus.

Do you want a friend who, when he's with you, is *with you*? A friend who treats you like you matter, like time with you is a priority and a joy? There's no friend so perfectly present as Jesus.

Do you want a friend who would take a bullet for you? A friend who would push you out of the way to take your place in front of an oncoming train? A friend who would walk into a buzzsaw for you? There is no friend—none in the world—so saving as Jesus.

Whenever you see a cross, remember it should've been you on there. But, praise God, it wasn't. Your friend Jesus said he'd take it for you.

If you've never reckoned with that amazing grace, I have no idea how you've gotten this far into this book, but I wouldn't want to conclude without urging you to turn from your sin and place your faith in him. He is real. He's glorious. He loves you. And he will save you. You can be forgiven forever and have eternal life with him. His work on the cross and out of that tomb can be yours. Don't waste another second knowing about him without actually knowing him. He won't refuse you.

If you have already come to know Jesus, I pray this book's been fuel for the furnace of your affections for him. It's a blessing sometimes just to be reminded of the age-old comforts of grace, isn't it?

He really does love us. And we really can know him.

Everything's a bit murky now. But day by day it's getting clearer. And someday soon(!), we'll look into his face, and we'll have no regrets for having followed him even throughout a long, hard life. All of that will fade away in the brightness of his person.

Until then, no matter where life finds us, if we look closely, we can see that light. "For God who said, 'Let light shine out of darkness,' has shone in our hearts to give the light of the knowledge of God's glory in the face of Jesus Christ" (2 Cor. 4:6).

Jesus is real. Even now, in our hearts, we can see his face.

ACKNOWLEDGMENTS

As I said in the introduction, this book is the culmination of years of struggles with lowness and celebrations of joy. In many ways, *Friendship with the Friend of Sinners* is the book I feel that I was born to write. And in many ways I feel very inadequate to write it. Somebody once said that writing a book about the Bible is like building a sandcastle at the base of Mount Everest. Well, writing a book about friendship with Jesus is like that too. Chapter by chapter, I racked my brain and ransacked my vocabulary to try to do some semblance of justice to the staggering possibility of intimacy with the Son of God.

Whether I succeeded in this endeavor is probably not for me to say, but I wouldn't have even tried without the constant encouragement of those who have championed the project of this book over the last year and a half—and those who've championed the project of me over the last forty-plus years! To name just a few from both categories:

My agent, Don Gates, has been an indefatigable advocate for my literary efforts. It's an incredible pleasure to do this kind of business with someone who gets the gospel and gets *me*.

Big thanks to all the folks at Baker Books, for whom this is my fourth book, especially editors Brian Vos and Lindsey Spoolstra. Thanks for taking chance after chance with me, and thanks for making the books better before they see the light of day.

My role at Midwestern Baptist Theological Seminary has brought me as close to a dream job as I ever could've hoped. I'm exceedingly grateful for Dr. Jason Allen, Dr. Jason Duesing, and all my friends and colleagues there for giving me a wide lane in which to write.

The congregation at Liberty Baptist Church is a joy to know and to pastor. My fellow pastors there are a constant encouragement and support system for me.

The ministry residents of the Pastoral Training Center at Liberty Baptist keep me honest and committed to seeing this stuff as a vital reality, not just as ministerial theory.

Some pastors who have given me reminders of the presence of Jesus include Ray Ortlund, Scotty Smith, David Pinckney, Jeff Dodge, and Steve Bezner.

This book couldn't have been written without the invaluable friendships throughout my life that have shown me incredible grace. These acknowledgments would be incomplete without mentioning David and Sarah McLemore, Ronnie and Melissa Martin, and those to whom this book has been dedicated, the Thinklings: Eric Guel, Mark Miranda, Bill Roberts, and Phil Schroeder. Thanks for putting up with me. Sorry I don't text more. I love you guys.

Second to last in this list, but second to first in my heart, is my wife, Becky, who hasn't just led me in cheer throughout the process of this book but has been a constant encourager and a happy comforter throughout all my life, and the best girlfriend a guy could have. Thank you, Beck. I love you more.

Finally, I want to give the utmost praise to the only wise God, Christ Jesus our Lord. I thank him for saving me. I thank him for not throwing me away. I thank him for just being who he is, which is all to me. Thank you, Jesus, for being a friend to a sinner like me.

NOTES

Chapter 1 Where Did Everybody Go?

1. Frederick Buechner, *Godric: A Novel* (New York: HarperCollins, 1980), 3.

2. Carl Trueman, *The Rise and Triumph of the Modern Self: Cultural Amnesia, Expressive Individualism, and the Road to Sexual Revolution* (Wheaton: Crossway, 2020).

3. *Tombstone*, written by Kevin Jarre, directed by George P. Cosmatos (Burbank, CA: Hollywood Pictures, 1993).

Chapter 2 Servants or Friends?

1. C. S. Lewis, "The Nativity," in *Poems* (San Diego: Harcourt Brace, 1992), 122.

2. Jared Wilson, *The Imperfect Disciple: Grace for People Who Can't Get Their Act Together* (Grand Rapids: Baker Books, 2017), 109–10.

Chapter 3 Nearer than Our Next Breath

1. Samuel Rutherford, *The Loveliness of Christ* (Carlisle, PA: Banner of Truth Trust, 2015), 26.

2. Katie Warren, "Japan Has Appointed a 'Minister of Loneliness' after Seeing Suicide Rates in the Country Increase for the First Time in 11 Years," *Insider*, February 22, 2021, https://www.insider.com/japan-minister-of-loneliness-suicides-rise-pandemic-2021-2.

3. Billy Baker, "The Biggest Threat Facing Middle-Age Men Isn't Smoking or Obesity. It's Loneliness," *Boston Globe*, March 9, 2017,

https://www.bostonglobe.com/magazine/2017/03/09/the-biggest-threat
-facing-middle-age-men-isn-smoking-obesity-loneliness/k6saC9FnnH
QCUbf5mJ8okL/story.html.

4. Samuel Rutherford, *Letters of Samuel Rutherford*, 3rd ed., edited
by Andrew A. Bonar (London: The Religious Tract Society), loc. 221,
https://www.gutenberg.org/files/42557/42557-h/42557-h.htm.

Chapter 4 On the Unsucking of Your Gut

1. Dietrich Bonhoeffer, *Life Together* (New York: Harper & Row,
1954), 111.

Chapter 5 Just Abide

1. Dallas Willard, *The Divine Conspiracy: Rediscovering Our Hidden
Life in God* (San Francisco: HarperCollins, 1998), 359.

Chapter 6 The Law against Double Jeopardy

1. Corrie ten Boom with Jamie Buckingham, *Tramp for the Lord* (Fort
Washington, PA: CLC Publications, 2011), 116.

2. This section of John's Gospel is contested, however, as it does not
appear in the earliest manuscripts. Indeed, it does not appear as part of
the corpus until about the fifth century. That's a good reason not to treat
it as canonical, but it could still be an authentic eyewitness account of
something that really happened. Our modern Bibles include it here in
John 8, though it has previously appeared in other parts of the Gospels,
usually with a footnote to the effect that it may not be authentic. It
certainly sounds like Jesus, though, doesn't it? In any event, it's a great
moment, historical or not. I mention it here not as being as authoritative as all the other Scripture references I'm citing in this book but as a
beautiful illustration of Christ's advocacy for the accused.

3. Joseph Medlicott Scriven, "What a Friend We Have in Jesus" (1855),
public domain.

Chapter 7 Shooting Straight

1. John Donne, "Holy Sonnet 14," in *The Poetry of Piety: An Anno-
tated Anthology of Christian Poetry*, edited by Ben Witherington III and
Christopher Mead Armitage (Grand Rapids: Baker Academic, 2002), 14.

Chapter 8 And the Kitchen Sink

1. John Bunyan, *Come and Welcome to Jesus Christ* (Carlisle, PA: Banner of Truth Trust, 2011), 85–86.

2. C. S. Lewis, *Mere Christianity* (Westwood, NJ: Barbour, 1952), 140.

Chapter 9 I Just Didn't Want You to Be Alone

1. Thomas Obediah Chisholm, "Great Is Thy Faithfulness" (1923), public domain.

2. J. Wilbur Chapman, "Jesus! What a Friend for Sinners!" (1910), public domain.

3. Athanasius, *On the Incarnation*, translated by John Behr (Yonkers, NY: SVS Press, 2012), 60.

Chapter 10 I Love You to Death

1. As quoted in J. I. Packer, "What Did the Cross Achieve? The Logic of Penal Substitution," Tyndale Biblical Theology Lecture, July 17, 1973, Tyndale House, Cambridge, http://www.the-highway.com/cross_Packer.html.

ABOUT THE AUTHOR

Jared C. Wilson is assistant professor of pastoral ministry and author in residence at Midwestern Seminary and director of the pastoral training center at Liberty Baptist Church, both in Kansas City, Missouri. He is the author of numerous books, including *The Imperfect Disciple*, *The Prodigal Church* (which won *World Magazine*'s Accessible Theology Book of the Year), *The Gospel According to Satan*, and *Love Me Anyway*. He is the host of the *For the Church* podcast and cohost of *Christianity Today*'s *The Art of Pastoring* podcast. Jared also blogs at the For the Church website, and he speaks at numerous churches and conferences around the world.